THE HISTORY

OF

THE FIRST BATTALION
THE LINCOLNSHIRE REGIMENT

IN

INDIA, ARAKAN, BURMA
and SUMATRA

●

The Naval & Military Press Ltd

SEPTEMBER 1939
TO
OCTOBER 1946

Published by

The Naval & Military Press Ltd

Unit 5 Riverside, Brambleside
Bellbrook Industrial Estate
Uckfield, East Sussex
TN22 1QQ England

Tel: +44 (0)1825 749494

www.naval-military-press.com
www.nmarchive.com

In reprinting in facsimile from the original, any imperfections are inevitably reproduced and the quality may fall short of modern type and cartographic standards.

The following story has been compiled from accounts supplied by Lieut. Col. C. A. C. Sinker, d.s.o. and Lieut. Col. D. P. St. C. Rossier, o.b.e. Some of the illustrations are from photographs supplied by the Imperial War Museum, London; others from snapshots lent by Major A. W. Innes, m.c., who also gave valuable advice and suggestions regarding the maps.

L. C. Gates, *Major*

late Royal Lincolnshire Regt.

Lincoln,

May, 1949.

CONTENTS.

FOREWORD BY
FIELD MARSHAL SIR WILLIAM SLIM,
G.B.E., K.C.B., D.S.O., M.C.

The campaign in Burma was predominantly an infantry-man's war. There he fought, not only against a tenacious and brutal enemy, but against country, climate and disease. This is a brief account of how one infantry battalion fought, endured, and conquered.

The 1st Battalion The Royal Lincolnshire Regiment, in an Army where there were many fine battalions, held a reputation second to none for those cardinal virtues of the British Infantryman—cheerfulness, steadiness, stubborn valour and a morale that never faltered.

W. J. Slim

F. M.

CHAPTER I

INDIA : 1939-1942.

When war broke out on September 3rd, 1939, the 1st Battalion The Lincolnshire Regiment was stationed at Nasirabad in Rajputana, with one Company on detachment at Ahmedabad in the Bombay Presidency.

Early in 1940, the Battalion moved to Dinapore in Bihar, with a company detachment at Muzzafapur. The 2nd Battalion had been stationed here several years before. The role of the Battalion in Dinapore was internal security, and Bihar was a province where civil disturbances were not infrequent. While here, "C" and "D" Companies spent a short period training in Ranchi, and helped to start what was later to become one of the biggest military stations in India. About the middle of 1940 the Battalion was ordered to stand by for a move to England, but this was cancelled, and later in the year we moved instead to Nowshera in the North West Frontier Province. Here we had to learn all about mountain warfare, which was quite new to most of us, and actually spent most of our time out of Nowshera on column or in camp. At this time the defences on the North Western Frontier on the Afghan border were being prepared, and the Battalion marched up through Peshawar and the Kyber Pass to Landi Kotal for a month's digging in that area.

The 1st Battalion of the Regiment at Nasirabad, Rajputana, March, 1939.

In 1941 trouble broke out among the tribesmen in Waziristan in the Tochi valley district and the Battalion was ordered to Razmak to take over garrison duties from the Queen's Royal Regiment, who were to take part in the column sent out to restore order. The Battalion was by this time fairly proficient in training for mountain warfare and, after two rehearsals with the Queen's, took over their part in the duty of opening the road from Razmak to Razmak Narai and Alexandra Fort on road opening days. The road was usually opened about three days in the week.

During the time that the Battalion was engaged in this work the tribesmen were on the whole quiet ; while we were in Razmak we had only two casualties, both of whom were wounded. When the trouble in the Tochi valley had been dealt with, the Queen's returned and the Battalion was relieved and moved back again to Nowshera, where we spent the Christmas of 1941.

About this time Lt. Colonel E. F. O. Richards, M.C., relinquished command on promotion to Brigadier and the Battalion was taken over by Lt. Colonel P. H. Gates. Brigadier G. G. C. Bull, O.B.E., had now taken over command of the Nowshera Brigade.

Early in 1942 the Battalion again marched up the Khyber Pass to Landi Kotal and continued to work on the construction of the North Western defences, this time living in a perimeter camp near the top of Spinet Suka, in intense cold.

After a few weeks' hard work in this area the Battalion was recalled to Nowshera as the Nowshera Brigade had been ordered to Bengal to meet the threat of a Japanese invasion.

After a short delay in Nowshera, the Battalion finally arrived at Diamond Harbour about thirty miles south of Calcutta on the Hoogly River. Diamond Harbour proved a disappointment to all, turning out to be a very small town on the banks of the river with no apparent harbour. The Battalion marched out a few miles to their new home the same day, to Hartugungh, a small Bengali village surrounded by paddy fields and jungle, where we stayed for the next few weeks.

After many recces and discussions, the Battalion finally moved a few miles to another cluster of Bengali villages at Deula, and here the Nowshera Brigade, now known as 71 Brigade, concentrated and formed a defensive area or "harbour," from where it was to be their role to send out columns to deal with any attempted Japanese invasions.

The Battalion was to spend almost a year in Deula, which was really a collection of small villages with a railway station on the Sealdah (Calcutta)-Diamond Harbour line. Work on the defences started at once, and the whole Brigade area was wired and platoon and Company posts constructed in depth. Most of the ground was paddy with patches of slightly higher ground on which were clusters of trees, usually palms, and native huts of mud and thatch. All the villagers were evacuated, and the Battalion took over their homes and very soon most of the houses were made comparatively clean and fairly comfortable. Ventilation was improved and beds were soon constructed out of bamboo. Some lived in tents.

The monsoon in East Bengal was new to all of us and we were very soon to learn our first lessons in the proper construction and drainage of defences in such an area and climate. Much of our earlier work proved to be useless and most defences had to be built up rather than dug down and in planning any defence work we learnt that a system of drainage must be one of the earliest considerations. The many hours spent later in baling out and re-revetting positions finally brought this home to us.

Apart from the work on the defences, the Brigade now started intensive training, jungle warfare being one of the main items. The Brigade now consisted of the 1st Lincolns, the 7 15th Punjab and the 9 15th Punjab. Both the Indian units were new and had only been raised during the war.

When the Battalion arrived in Bengal from the North West Frontier Province, we were as fit as it was possible for a battalion to be ; our many long marches and hard digging in a healthy climate were responsible for this. The heat and humidity of the new area soon began to have a bad effect, and the number of sick started to assume rather alarming proportions. A great deal of this was due to skin diseases in the form of boils, impetigo, jungle sores and ringworm. Malaria at this time was not such a common disease as it was to become later on. By way of relaxation all ranks were allowed into Calcutta for thirty-six hours every month which made a small break which was very much appreciated.

A large draft of East Surreys now joined us, later to be known as the "thirsty" draft because, being new to the climate, their consumption of water to begin with was quite abnormal. Their officers and men gradually became absorbed and became " Lincolns," and served with the Battalion until those that remained were repatriated towards the end of the war. They were a fine draft and in time found three Company Commanders and many of the higher non-commissioned ranks.

We were in Deula for the Cyclone in 1942. One of the detachments at Kulpe on the banks of the Hoogly was completely washed out, and was lucky to escape with the loss of only one mule. An enormous amount of damage was done in the district.

We were also in Deula when the riots or rebellion of 1942 started, and "A" Company, Major Hill, and " D " Company, Major Sinker, were sent out across the Hoogly to help to restore order in the Midnapore district. " D " Company were forced to open fire on one occasion when, having occupied a building that turned out to be a Congress Headquarters, they were surrounded by a mob some thousands strong who were slowly closing in and refused to disperse.   When the looting and rioting had been quelled, the two Companies returned again to Deula.

Major S. A. Cooke, the Second in Command, left soon after this to take command of a Battalion of The King's Regiment.

71 Brigade was now part of 26 Indian Division commanded by General Haywood ; collective and individual training, always combined with the constant upkeep and repair of defences, was intensified.   Before long Brigadier Bull was able to report that 71 Brigade was in all ways fit for war.

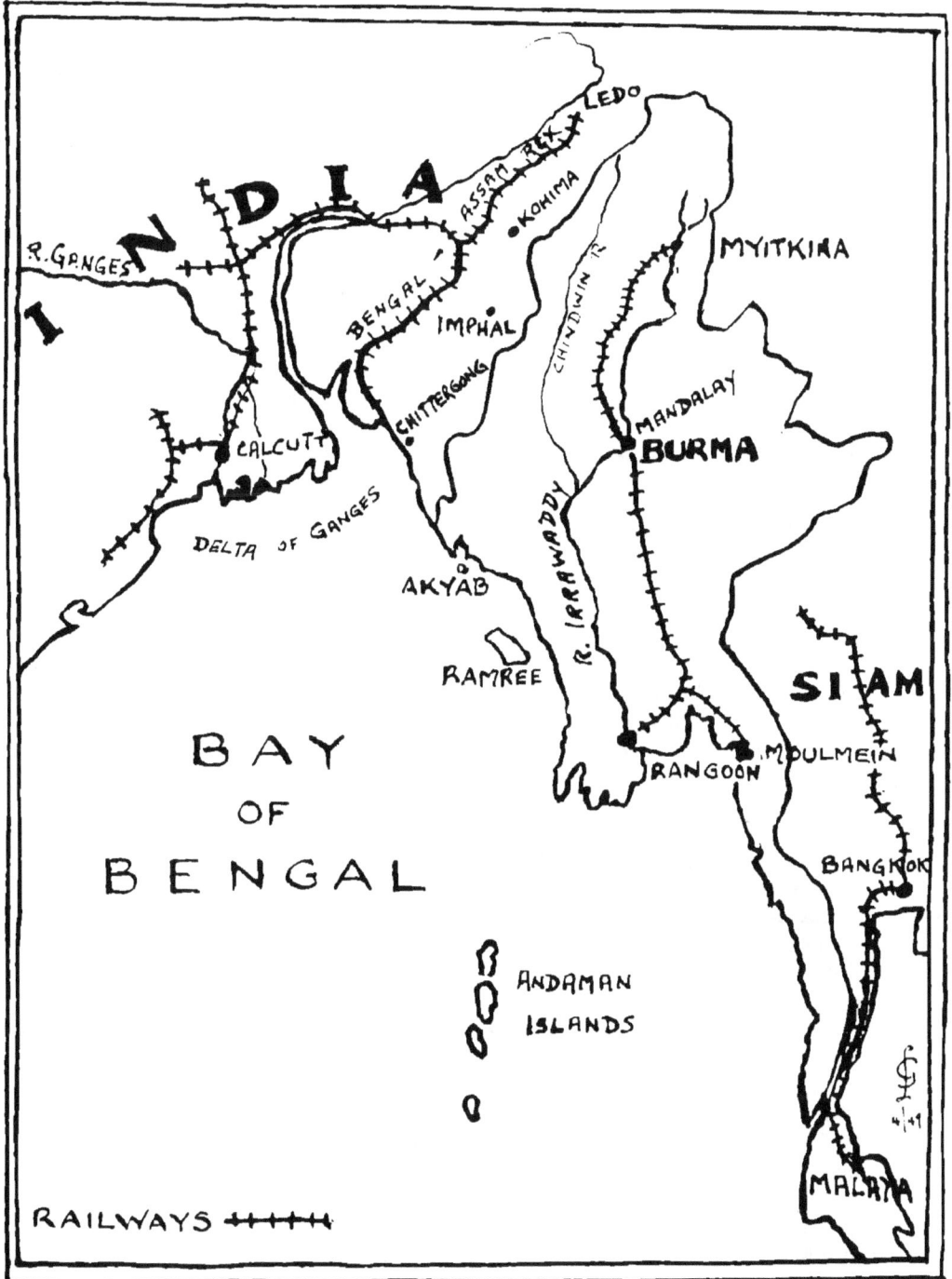

CHAPTER II

EARLY DAYS IN THE ARAKAN AND THE ACTION AT DONBAIK.

(See Map 2 at end of Chapter).

Early in 1943 reinforcements were required by 14 Division in the Arakan and 71 Brigade were selected from 26 Division to move. The Brigade moved early in February via Calcutta and Chittagong to Maungdaw. At Chittagong mosquito nets and pith helmets were withdrawn, and steel helmets were worn for the future.

The Japanese at this time held Akyab Island, and on the Mayu Peninsula, Rathidaung on the east of the range and Donbaik on the west.

The Arakan, which in time the Battalion was to get to know so well, was different from the country round Deula in that it was more densely wooded with thicker jungle and less paddy. The country was also hilly, rising in places to over a thousand feet. The Deula area had been completely flat.

All the main features in the Arakan run north and south, the main hill features being the Mayu Range, which runs in an unbroken line from Foul Point, opposite Akyab Island in the south, past Maungdaw and Bawli Bazaar, and north throughout the Arakan. The highest peak on the range is about fifteen hundred feet. The width of the range and its jungle clad slopes varies and is about six miles between Bawli Bazaar and Goppe Bazaar in the north, dwindling down to nothing at Foul Point in the south, a distance of about sixty miles. West of the range the ground becomes flat and consists of paddy, scrub and a few villages leading down to the sea or further north to the Naaf River, the mouth of which is just south of Maungdaw. Across the Naaf River is the Teknaf Peninsula which is bordered by the sea to the west. A range of hills again runs up the middle of this peninsula from Teknaf in the south, opposite Maungdaw, past Nhila and Timbru Ghat in the north. East of the Mayu Range the country is comparatively flat, interspersed with many hills rising to about three hundred feet, and down the centre runs the Kalapanzin River, through Goppe Bazaar to Buthidaung, south of which it becomes the Mayu River past Rathedaung to the sea. East of the river, after much of the same sort of country, is another high range of hills which slope down in the east to the Kaladan River. The whole "grain" of the country thus runs north and south, intersected by streams, locally known as Chaungs, of varying sizes running east and west from the ranges into the rivers or sea. Some of these chaungs are unfordable throughout the year, and many more become so during the monsoon.

In 1943 there was only one road across the Mayu Range between Maungdaw and Buthidaung, which went through two narrow tunnels. There were three tracks across, which could be made muleable, at Indin, Ngaukeydauk and Goppe. The last two were made passable to mules in 1943 and to motor transport in 1944. There were no bridges across the Naaf, the Kalapanzin or Mayu Rivers.

The only all-weather road in the area was between Maungdaw and Buthidaung. Motorable dry weather tracks ran from Bawli Bazaar via Maungdaw to Donbaik and from Buthidaung to Rathidaung. All the hills were covered in jungle, or if not were very high in scrub. Most of the open country had at some time been cultivated with paddy. The jungle everywhere was very thick and really only passable along chaungs, paths or game tracks. It was possible to cut a way through, but this was noisy, exhausting and very slow.

The climate was not unpleasant, though at times very hot. In the dry season it was very dry and very dusty especially as more motor transport arrived, and in the wet season it was very wet and very muddy. Nearly all the flat country, land that had once been cultivated, was at least a foot under water in the rains. In the dry season the nights were cold and there was usually a ground mist in the mornings.

There were swarms of flies and mosquitoes and the Arakan was one of the worst malarial areas in the world.

At this time there were very few local inhabitants as most of them had moved north to get out of the danger zone. Those that remained appeared to be friendly.

In this country the 1st Battalion arrived in the middle of February, 1943, and disembarked from river steamers at Maungdaw from where we set off on our march south. At Indin after a trying march of about twenty miles, done by night, when it was cool and safer from interference from Japanese aircraft, the Battalion advance party and Advanced Brigade Headquarters were caught up with, and we went into "harbour."

At Indin many heard their first sounds of battle when they heard the guns firing on the positions near Donbaik to the south. The Battalion was able to put in a few more days' battle practice and battle inoculation, while the Commanding Officer took small parties forward to reconnoitre future positions. At Indin we had our first casualty when one of the signallers, Pte. King, was bitten by a snake. He was rushed to the Regimental Aid Post, where Captain Craig, the Medical Officer, had anti-snake bite serum and gave him injections. Pte. King, though away from the Battalion for some time, finally recovered and came back to us.

On February 21st the Battalion moved forward, again by night, to an assembly area and on the 22nd took over a part of the line from the Royal Inniskilling Fusiliers. The line ran from the foothills of the Mayu Range to the sea, a distance of about one mile which was held by two Battalions. The Lincolns were on the right with their right on the beach and the 7 15th Punjab were on the left.

Little was known of how the Japs held the area or in what strength, but several frontal attacks had been made with heavy artillery support, resulting in heavy losses to our troops.

The Inniskillings had made two such attacks and were consequently very under-strength. They were also very tired as they had been continually in action without rest for many weeks. Looking out from our front posts, in a chaung running down to the sea, we could see the bodies of about a platoon of them still lying in the open where they had been caught in enfilade by the enemy.

The whole area had been well fought over and consequently was insanitary and unpleasant. Only the sea looked inviting, stretching unbroken to the horizon in the Bay of Bengal in the west, a sparkling blue, relieved only in the distance to the south west by the lighthouse on Oyster Island.

The Battalion settled down very quickly and were remarkably steady in their fire discipline and control. The strangeness of the nights in the jungle opposed to the Japs was new to all and naturally a little nerve wracking. The enemy probably realised this and made full use of his red tracer and some form of bullets that exploded with a crack in, or well behind our lines.

Two Battalions held the front while one rested. Each Battalion had an administrative area, in our case known as " Tamil," just behind the lines, where necessary stores were kept with a rear Headquarters under the Second in Command. All the Battalion cooking was done in this area, and hot meals were carried forward after dark by hand or where possible by mule. No cooking could be done in the forward areas. As no oil was available, the smoke of the fires frequently brought down Jap gunfire, and from this we suffered our first battle casualty when Lieut. Greenshields, of " D " Company, was killed near the Company cooking area.

The enemy held the high ground on the Mayu Range to the south and could overlook our positions and must have been able to watch a good deal of movement in our lines. We could never see anything of them though we could see several of their positions.

Enemy identifications were required and a carefully planned raid by a part of " C " Company supported by artillery was carried out. The raiding party got into the Jap lines known as " The Chaung" to find only the dead and rotting bodies of previous attackers. A certain amount of useful topographical information was obtained.

It was about this time that the Commanding Officer, Colonel Gates, had a narrow escape when some shells burst on Battalion Headquarters near his slit trench when he was shaving and he was hit by several splinters from the trees.

Battalion Headquarters moved to another patch of jungle the same morning where they were left in peace.

The enemy were either very short of or very careful with their artillery ammunition, but when they did open fire their shells were usually well placed and frequently caused damage. However, we soon got to know the different sounds and when our own guns were not firing often had time to take cover before the arrival of enemy shells. We had at least a Regiment of 25 pounders and a battery or two of 3.7's in support with a very generous supply of ammunition. Against all this fire power the Jap positions appeared to remain intact. At this time our knowledge of Japanese earthworks and "bunkers" was very limited and there were many fantastic stories current of underground tunnels and forts.

The Battalion moved back after a time to rest, and a patrol was sent out from "A" Company under Captain Wright to try and work round to the left through the jungle on the Mayu Range. When moving along a small chaung they ran into a Jap machine gun post. The leading men were killed and two enemy were also killed. The remainder of the patrol got back, but with little information and one man missing. Two days later the missing man returned. He had been captured by the enemy and taken back to their post Headquarters. Here his rifle was taken away from him and his boots were removed, but he was left with his bayonet and a grenade. No one seemed to take much notice of him and no one gave him any food. During the night he got tired of this and decided to try and slip away. He was successful in this and after many long hours' wandering about barefooted in the jungle found his way home, very tired, very footsore but very happy.

The Battalion moved up into the line again, this time on the left, holding a ridge known as Twin Knobs ; Tamil remained in the same position. Twin Knobs was a spur running north and south among the foothills of the Mayu Range and at the southern end the enemy positions and our own were only a few yards apart. The ridge jutted into and behind part of the Jap lines and afforded a very good view of the whole of the country round about the village of Donbaik. In its turn the whole of Twin Knobs was overlooked by Jap positions to the southeast on the top of the Mayu Range on Point 836. The ridge was mostly covered in thick jungle, largely bamboo, which afforded good cover from view but gave very limited fields of fire. Regimental Aid Post was in a chaung at the north end of the ridge, the same chaung that was held by the Japs further to the west towards the sea.

It was on Twin Knobs one day that Sgt. Willcox of the mortar Platoon met a fourteen foot python. Scarcely able to believe his eyes, but informed by his pal that there was some more of it round the corner, he managed to shoot it with his tommy gun. With much labour it was dragged down to the Regimental Aid Post where the Medical Officer was asked to provide a bottle in which to preserve it !

Towards the middle of March, Higher Command decided that a really determined effort must be made to drive the Japanese off the Mayu Peninsula before the arrival of the monsoon.

For this purpose 6 Independent Brigade was sent down to Donbaik. This Brigade, which consisted of four regular British Battalions—the Royal Scots, Royal Berkshire, Royal Welsh and the D.L.I. were splendidly equipped and very highly trained in combined operations on which they had been concentrating for about two years. The Brigade was commanded by Brigadier Cavendish who was later captured and killed whilst in Japanese hands, probably by our own guns.

The Lincolns now left 71 Brigade for a short time and came under command of 6 Independent Brigade and a combined attack with the five Battalions on the Japanese positions was planned. During this time the Battalion withdrew for a short rest being relieved by the Royal Scots. A few days later we re-occupied our positions on Twin Knobs from which we took our part in the operation.

Major Innes who commanded "A" Company in the action of Donbaik writes the following account :—

"After days of planning and rehearsing we were told that " D " Day for the attack on the Jap main defence line at Donbaik was to be the 18th March.

10

The position had been attempted twice before without success and the results of those two attacks had lain in front of our position for three weeks. Those bodies of the Inniskillings and Indian troops from the Brigade we had taken over from, were grim reminders of Jap tenacity and their Donbaik defences. By this time we knew the Donbaik position well. Oddly enough, very few of us could admit to having seen a Jap, but we had all had our daily doses from his small arms and mortar fire.

" On the 16th March we were occupying a position called ' Twin Knobs.' This was a bamboo covered saddle overlooking the famous ' Chaung,' held by the Japs, and in its turn overlooked by the main Mayu Range, also held by the Japs. It was part of a range of foothills running from north to south, and twenty yards south of our forward section posts the Japs occupied their most northerly positions.

" The whole Jap defence line from the sea to the foothills of the Mayu range was to be pierced by 6 British Infantry Brigade with 1st Lincolns under command to make the Brigade up to five battalions. We were to attack the Jap positions on the extreme left of the line directly forward of ' Twin Knobs.' The attack was to be preceded by an artillery deception plan followed by a creeping barrage to cover our advance to the objective, some 800 yards south. During our advance on the objective we were to bye-pass known Jap positions and having consolidated to attack north, back towards ' Twin Knobs.' This was to be carried out by ' A,' ' B,' and ' C ' Companies, while ' D ' Company was to be held in reserve to attack south from ' Twin Knobs ' if required. It was intended that by nightfall the Jap defences between our position on ' Twin Knobs ' and our objective, should be cleaned up to allow the next stage of the Brigade plan to become operative.

" By the evening of the 17th March we had had our final orders. ' B ' and ' C ' Companies were to advance to the objective along a chaung running north and south, east of ' Twin Knobs,' and 'A' Company through the low-lying jungle on the west of ' Twin Knobs.' By supper time we had withdrawn from our forward positions on ' Twin Knobs,' and these had been taken over by a Company of the Royal Scots. Our makeshift positions for the night were in the main chaung north of ' Twin Knobs,' for here we were immune from Jap small arms fire.

" Just before dusk, Col. Gates came round to the Companies and spoke to each section. His advice and encouragement at that moment was just what we wanted, for this was our first attack since the outbreak of war and he was the only man in the Battalion with previous battle experience. We all had that empty feeling and wondered whether 24 hours would see us in Heaven or Hell or even still swatting mosquitoes in the Arakan jungle.

" No one overslept that night for in the early hours of the morning on 18th March, shells were whistling over our heads both ways. The cooks produced an excellent hot breakfast from their jungle cookhouses swathed in blankets to hide the flames. 'A' Company's chief ' food moaner ' was for once at a loss to find anything to grumble about. Accepting the meal as the ' best ever ' he concluded by announcing that it was only ' cannon fodder.'

"Any attempt to maintain our sense of humour was soon broken by a very alarming explosion in our 3-inch mortar position, to be followed by a call for stretcher bearers and a sad party of men bearing the killed and wounded back to the Regimental Aid Post. The Japs had scored a ' direct ' hit. The waiting was unpleasant and we were thankful when we moved up to the starting line. Our barrage was standing on its start line and we were glad that we were on the right side of it.

"At ' H ' hour we were off. Keeping up to the barrage in the jungle where shells were touching off in the trees, kept us fully occupied. At last we could unleash our energy, and 'A,' ' B ' and ' C ' Companies lost no time in getting to the other end. We all had some difficulty in finding the way but to our astonishment the Japs left us alone. Half an hour later we had all arrived on the objective with the feeling that attacks weren't so bad after all. We had had no casualties.

" The Commanding Officer had given orders that on arrival the three Company Commanders should confer as to the best method of mopping up, but that ' C ' Company would do the job if intact, while 'A' and ' B ' consolidated. After a further ' O ' group attended by Major Hocquard, Major Hoey and Major Innes, commanding ' C,' ' B ' and 'A' Companies respectively, Major Hocquard decided that ' C ' Company should attack north and mop up. A delay occurred and it was almost an hour before ' C ' Company were on the move.

" It was from then on that the battle really started. The Commanding Officer had ordered ' D ' Company under Major Hill to follow the route of 'A' Company and attack the ridge at an intermediate point between the start line and the point reached by ' B ' and 'A' Companies.

" Both ' D ' and ' C ' Companies found themselves confronted by a succession of stubborn Japanese section posts dug in on the top of the spur we had bye-passed. From approximately 10.00 hours until 17.00 hours the Japs were attacked again and again but could not be reached. Our casualties mounted as ' D ' Company tried to overcome the Japs. Major Hill persisted with his assaults, each time to reach the top of the spur but only to be swept off by a hail of Jap grenades and bullets. At about midday, the situation between ' Twin Knobs' and the objective which by then had been consolidated, became confused. Wireless sets had been knocked out and lines cut. Those who were present will never forget the familiar sound of Col. Gates's voice booming across the jungle in an attempt to establish contact with his fighting Companies. He had moved forward from his command post leaving Captain Cotton, the Adjutant, to deal with any messages that came in. In the afternoon communications were working again, and forward Companies were told that ' D ' Company's attack had stopped and both ' D ' and ' C ' were to hold on to their positions while 'A' and ' B ' were to remain on the objective.

" In spite of our difficulties we were now full of confidence. We had gained our objective and we very definitely knew where the Japs were. With the aid of artillery and mortars we knew that we could overcome them.

" By this time, however, we were all very tired and short of water. Our bottles had been filled before we started but the Arakan in March was hot, to say the least, and eight hours' fighting and digging did nothing to lessen our thirst. However, arrangements were being made to send up packhals and we hoped by nightfall we would get a drink.

" It was towards 1600 hours when the Commanding Officer spoke to Major Innes on the wireless and told him to prepare to withdraw. Both he and Major Hoey tried to dissuade the Commanding Officer only to be told that orders had come from higher up. It transpired that the Brigade attack had been halted elsewhere and there was nothing left but to withdraw to our original positions. Although we were tired and thirsty this news was received with bitter disappointment by every man. There was nothing left but to obey orders and the plan for our withdrawal was laid on. The Japs knew where we were and we realised that to return to our positions would involve sneaking through the Jap lines. A move in thick jungle by night can only be accomplished in one way—single file. Orders were given and Major Innes with 'A' Company was to lead with ' C ' Company and their several casualties in the centre while Major Hoey was to bring up the rear with ' B ' Company.

"As soon as it was dark we started. There was no track, nothing but thick jungle ; a compass and the north star was our only guide. Every yard of jungle had to be cut, for a distance of 800 yards. More than half-a-dozen men were being carried on stretchers and we knew that if we were heard we would be dog's meat in no time.

" Only once during our six hour trek homeward did we despair. Having lost direction for about the tenth time we found ourselves in a dark, deep, unfriendly chaung, which appeared to be a 'cul de sac.' The column was halted and the leading Company Commander went forward with two men to reconnoitre. Twenty yards forward they stumbled across five glistening bayonets in the moonlight. Frozen to the ground they were suddenly welcomed by ' It's only us, Sir'—from a section of ' D ' Company. No sweeter sound had been heard all day. Contact had been made. Eventually after another two hours we recognised ' home ground ' and reported in.

" So ended our first real battle. We had done what had been expected of us and our eventual withdrawal was caused by circumstances beyond our control. We were not dispirited, in fact we were elated with the knowledge that we had now been in a real attack."

The following afternoon the Battalion withdrew and concentrated in the administrativ e area. The Battalion was very tired and disappointed at being forced to withdraw after their successful capture of their objective. The situation, however, east of the Mayu Range was now causing anxiety after the Jap break-through at Htizwe, north of Rathidaung, and reinforcements were urgently required on that side. Motor transport was provided and the Battalion embussed throughout the night and moved north to Maungdaw and then east through the Tunnels over the Mayu Range and assembled again a few miles west of Buthidaung, on the Letwedhet chaung below Point 551. Here the Battalion again came under command of 71 Brigade which was now joined by 4 Brigade, both being in Mayforce under command of Brigadier Curtis.

SECRET.

SPECIAL ORDER OF THE DAY

BY

LIEUTENANT COLONEL P. H. GATES,

COMMANDING

1st BATTALION THE LINCOLNSHIRE REGIMENT.

I have received the following letter from Brigadier R. V. C. Cavendish, O.B.E., M.C., Commander, 6th Infantry Brigade Group.

" I am writing this short letter to thank you and your Bn. for the very gallant part they took in yesterday's operation.

" It was with very deep regret that I had to recall your forward companies after they had gained their objectives. This, as you know, I was forced to do owing to the circumstances on other parts of our front.

" I should like to convey to you and the Officers and men of the Battalion my very great sorrow at the loss of so many brave men you sustained.

" I am only sorry that you and your battalion remained with us for such a short time. It was a great honour to me to be given them and I would like you to know how much I and my Staff appreciated the wonderful spirit of co-operation and willingness which we received from you.

" I should be very grateful if you would convey these rather badly expressed but very honest sentiments to the Officers and men. With best wishes and all good luck to you and your fine Battalion.

Yours sincerely,

Sd—R. V. CAVENDISH,

Brigadier.

Since writing the above I have been visited by the Army Commander and his Excellency The Commander-in-Chief, to whom I described the action. They wished me to convey their sorrow at your losses and congratulations on the way the Battalion fought."

I wish to thank all ranks of the Battalion for the fine work which earned this congratulatory letter. Such work is made possible only by the Leadership of all Company, Platoon and Section Commanders, combined with the determination and devotion to duty of all ranks. Such a letter must make every member of the Battalion not only proud but the more determined to uphold the traditions of the Regiment which have been handed down to us for 258 years.

P. H. GATES, *Lieutenant Colonel.*

Commanding 1st Battalion The Lincolnshire Regiment.

Field.
22 Mar. 43.

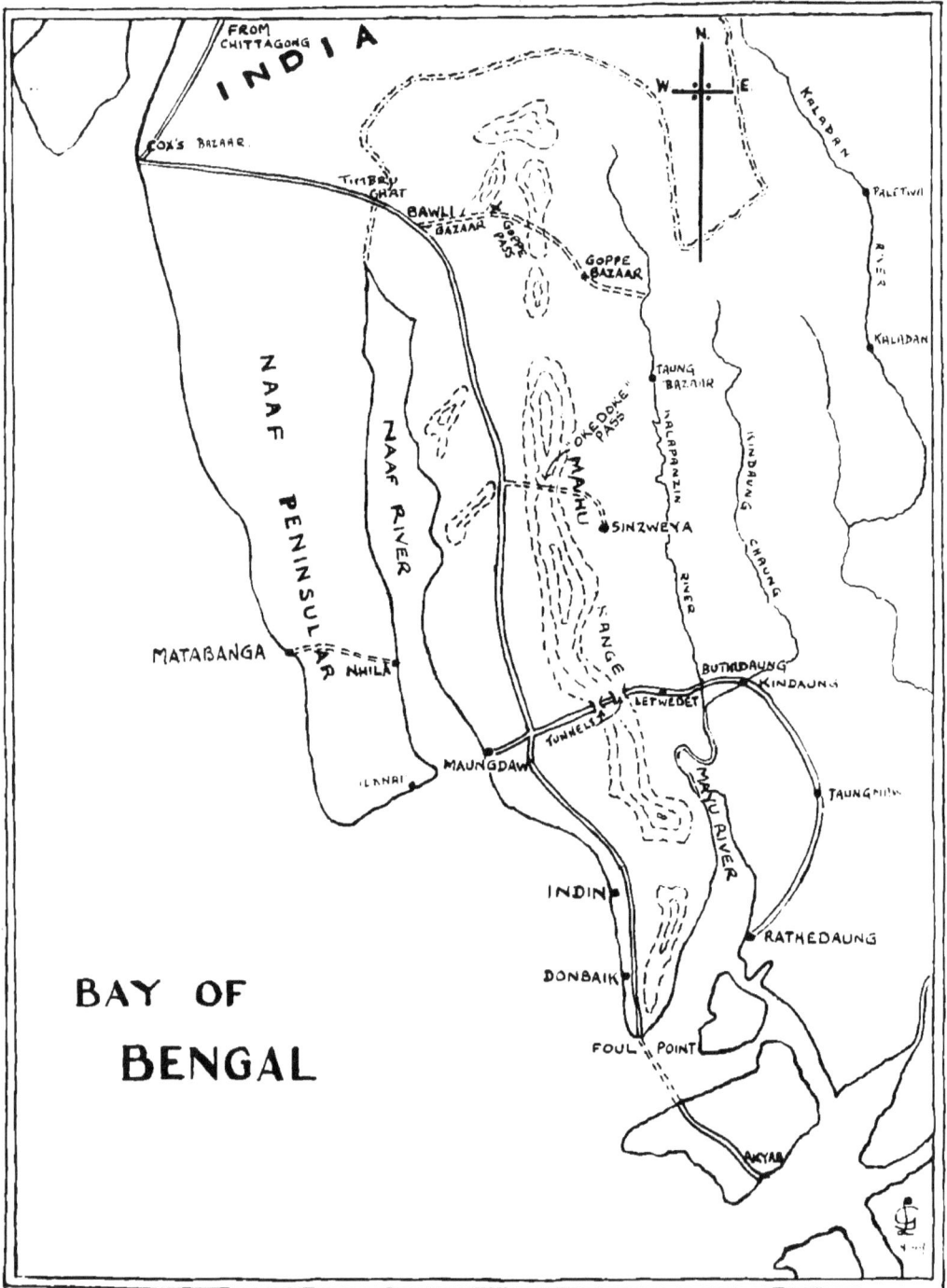

FROM CHITTAGONG

I N D I A

N

W E

KALADAN RIVER

COX'S BAZAAR

PALETWA

TIMBRU GHAT

BAWLI BAZAAR

GOPPE PASS

GOPPE BAZAAR

KHLADAN

N
A
A
F

P
E
N
I
N
S
U
L
A
R

N
A
A
F

R
I
V
E
R

TAUNG BAZAAR

OKEDOKE PASS

M
A
Y
U

KALAPANZIN RIVER

KINDAUNG CHAUNG

SINZWEYA

R
A
N
G
E

MATABANGA

NHILA

BUTHIDAUNG

KINDAUNG

LETWEDET

TUNNELS

MAUNGDAW

ILANRI

MAYU RIVER

TAUNGMAW

INDIN

RATHEDAUNG

DONBAIK

BAY OF
BENGAL

FOUL POINT

AKYAB

14

CHAPTER III

EAST OF THE MAYU RANGE.

The Battalion had a very short rest in the Letwedhet area and was able to wash bodies and clothes in the chaung and to reorganise as many had been lost through battle casualties and sickness. While resting the Battalion was visited by General Wavell, the Commander in Chief, and General Irwin, the G.O.C. in C., Eastern Command, who had commanded two battalions of the Lincolnshire Regiment in 1917 and 1918. Here also we were at last allowed to dump our Anti-gas Kit, which completely filled up about three three-ton lorries. This was later moved back to Maungdaw and never seen again as a Japanese aircraft very kindly scored a direct hit with a bomb. The men left in charge were luckily away at the time. The amount of kit carried around by the Battalion at this time was quite fantastic, the most heart-breaking load being about twenty tons of first line reserve ammunition.

After a couple of days the Battalion again moved into harbour just south of Buthidaung to an area known later as the "orchard." Here orders were received to move south, about twenty miles, across the Mayu River to a position in support of the 7/15th and 9/15th in the vicinity of the Aungtha Chaung. The Battalion moved by march route. All stores including the twenty tons of ammunition had to be loaded into lorries at the harbour, unloaded again at Buthidaung to be taken across the river in ferries and loaded again at the other side. Eight miles further south this loading and unloading had to be repeated in order to get across the Chaung at Kingdaung. In addition to all the loads, fifty-two Battalion mules and well over a hundred attached mules had to be ferried across the rivers.

The Battalion arrived at the Aungtha Chaung and took over from a Punjab Battalion commanded by Lt. Colonel Lowther, who was shortly to become Brigadier in command of 4 Brigade.

Just previous to this the Japanese had carried out an encircling movement, infiltrating through the jungle and launched a successful attack at Htziwi in rear of our troops facing Rathidaung. This had been followed by a withdrawal of our troops to an area about Taung-maw. The whole of our left flank was exposed to this form of attack and in our new position companies and platoons were placed in all the main chaungs leading from east to west across the Kingdaung Rathidaung road, including the Mraw Chaung about four miles north of the Aungtha Chaung. Patrolling was very active but practically no contact was made with the enemy. Captain Wright was the only casualty at this time, wounded in the arm in the Mraw Chaung by a small enemy patrol.

It was now decided, mainly by way of a diversion, to attack the Japanese slightly to the south of our position, on a feature known as Point 201. " A " and " B " Companies were selected and Major Innes commanding "A" Company writes the following account of the action :—

" Things were rather quiet for the Battalion. We were holding a position several miles behind the Taungmaw front in case the Japs tried a swinger on us—more than a probability than a possibility in the jungle. The Battalion was in the Aungtha Chaung with "A" Company a few miles to the north in the Mraw Chaung.

The Japs had been all too active in the Arakan and the latest news was that Tenabashi had crossed the Kalapanzin river from east to west and had cut across the Mayu Range to Indin, making things very uncomfortable for 6 Brigade who had had to pull out of Donbaik. A diversion was required and Division decided that an effort against the Japs at Taungmaw might make Tanabashi think twice before he continued northwards.

" It was eventually decided that an attack should be launched against the Jap position, on hill 201, south-west of Taungmaw. The object of the attack was not to gain ground but to hit the Japs hard and wake him up.

" The Taungmaw front was being held by the two Indian Battalions in the Brigade and the Brigadier therefore decided that we would do the attack while the 9 15 Punjab would come half-way to establish a firm base. As the attack was to be a limited one only two Companies were to be used, "A" and " B " were chosen with the usual specialists from Headquarters Company. The Commanding Officer would conduct the operation with a Tactical Head-quarters.

" Two or three days were spent in reconnaissance, always an arduous pastime in the Arakan as most of it had to be done on foot. We were very fortunate in being able to use an excellent observation post held by the 9 15 Punjab which enabled us to choose our route to the objective and plan in detail.

" The plan was roughly as follows : in the early hours of the night 17th/18th April, troops of the 9/15th were to move across no man's land (approximately 2000 yards) and establish a firm base 800 yards west of ' 201.' This would facilitate the later move of our force and ensure that no Japs would hamper our move to the objective and blow the gaff.

" Later on in the night we were to move out of our temporary harbour and cross no man's land. " B " Company was to occupy a feature approximately 500 yards west of "201 ' and finally "A" Company with a platoon of " D " Company under command was to pass through and assault ' 201 ' itself. It was known that the Japs occupied ' 201 " but there was no indication of their strength.

" On the evening of 16th April, Battalion Headquarters and "A" and " B " Companies moved forward to a temporary harbour area just behind the 9 15th forward positions about 1000 yards north of ' 201.' Although the country was open here we were well concealed by hills. The next day, the 17th April, was spent in final reconnaissance by platoon and section commanders and all N.C.O.s were given a chance of studying the route for the night march and viewing the objective. That evening the weather was unkind to us and a downpour of rain lasting for two or three hours literally dampened ourselves and our spirits as we were without any cover. Eventually ' H ' hour arrived and we moved off in column, once again in single file. Major Hoey led with " B " Company, followed by "A" Company, the rear being brought up by the I.O. and Battalion Headquarters. We were heavily laden as mules had to be left behind owing to two chaungs en route. The night march itself will long be remembered. We lost our way several times and found ourselves baulked by the first chaung which although dry contained several feet of soft mud. After what seemed eternity we made it and then completed a second crossing with the aid of assault boats. Fortunately sufficient time had been allowed for delays. Timings worked out just right and at approximately 0430 hours 'A" Company had reached the foot of ' 201 ' unseen, and, we hoped, unheard. 'A' Company had to wait until dawn for the assault. The early hours of the morning in the Arakan can be as cold as the midday sun is hot. Everyone was wet through by then, but the fact that we had accomplished Stage 1 of the operation put us in high spirits.

"At dawn we assaulted. A careful movement using the 'approved fire and movement' method proved unnecessary. On reaching the first false crest about half-way up we found ourselves unopposed. Company Headquarters and two platoons of 'A' Company occupied the position, Sergt. Boyle's platoon and C.S.M. Maughan with " B " Company's platoon were sent forward to occupy a feature on the same ridge as the crest of ' 201' but in rear. This entailed a movement through very thick jungle, dropping into a re-entrant and climbing again. After forty-five minutes they were seen on their objective. Still no sound from the enemy and we began to think that they had flown. A reconnoitring patrol was despatched to the crest of ' 201 ' and very soon returned to report ' booby traps and sounds of voices.' Major Innes then decided to move a platoon on to the crest of ' 201 ' and subsequently to investigate the voices. The platoon in position and ready for anything that might come their way, Major Innes, his company cook—Pte. Brown (who was commanding a section) and two others went forward with Tommy Guns to investigate.

" The voices turned out to be a Jap section post breakfasting. They were rapidly dealt with by four Tommy Guns and a handful of grenades. At once the alarm was raised. Japs began to run in all directions to man their posts. For half an hour practically every man in the Company was embroiled in the ' fire fight.' It was reckoned that during that time at least twenty Japs were accounted for. We now realised that the Japs occupied ' 201 ' with approximately a Company plus, and we had come to rest right amongst them. Such a situation is a frequent occurrence in jungle warfare.

" By 1000 hours things quietened down. We had accurate knowledge of at least five enemy positions and they knew where we were. Having caused considerable casualties and created alarm and despondency, 'A' Company decided to hold on to its positions. The Japs in their turn were determined that we should not be allowed to move. Fortunately we had a reasonably covered line of communication to ' B ' Company and were able to evacuate our wounded, five in all. Unfortunately two platoon commanders, Sgt. Young and Cpl. Hilkin were both hit. Sgt. Young had a miraculous escape when a Jap bullet passed through his neck.

" The next three hours were spent in hard digging under unpleasant conditions. The Japs were out for our blood and sniped us every time we moved. Everything was used to complete our position by dark—tools, forks and even finger nails. There was no need to remind anyone to keep down—the Japs relieved officers and N.C.O.s of that responsibility. Considerable difficulty was experienced in communicating with our other two platoons who were firmly established on a neighbouring hill. Handkerchiefs on sticks were resorted to— an excellent target for Jap snipers who took every advantage.

" By mid afternoon things had quietened down somewhat. Our artillery was playing up well with individual 'stonks' at Jap positions. This proved rather unhealthy for us as we were right amongst the Japs. At about 1500 hours the Commanding Officer and Brigadier were on the 'phone to Officer Commanding 'A' Company, hatching a plot for the resumption of the assault on ' 201.' Major Innes was convinced that no useful purpose could be attained by such an operation and his decision was abided by. This turned out to be just as well, for at 1600 hours a message came through from the Commanding Officer to say that the Battalion had received orders to withdraw to Buthidaung the next day. This meant that 'A' Company would have to extricate itself from ' 201 ' that evening and the whole Battalion withdraw that night. Withdrawal would be tricky. The Japs knew our every position and 'A' Company had to get out. If it was left too late there was a danger of losing direction and becoming embroiled in the dark.

" Within 'A' Company, plans were laid on to withdraw half-an-hour after dusk. The two furthest platoons were to come off their hill, through the Jap position and join the remainder of 'A' Company on their hill. Artillery, machine guns and every supporting weapon in 'A' Company were to blaze away for fifteen minutes to support this. All this had to be tied up with Sergt. Boyle and C.S.M. Maughan whose platoons were on the far hill, again with handkerchief signalling.

" ' H ' hour for the withdrawal arrived, and for fifteen minutes hell was let loose. The effectiveness of our covering fire was borne out by the fact that the Japs, who must have been fully aware of the movement, never fired and 'A' Company was able to concentrate without any casualties. Withdrawal was slow as 'A' Company had to move back by bounds, covering each other as they went. Eventually they extracted themselves and rejoined ' B ' Company and the remainder of the Battalion.

" The march back that night was no less uncomfortable than the march up the night before.

" Once again although we had to withdraw, through circumstances out of our control, we were in high spirits having hit the Japs hard. This type of 'tip and run' operation was to become a regular feature in our fighting in the Arakan as will be read later on. We reckoned we were getting fairly good at it, but ached to be part of a larger force and throw the Japs out of the Arakan for good and all."

As soon as the action at Point 201 was over the Battalion was suddenly ordered back to Buthidaung to come under command of 4 Brigade. This meant moving all the stores and mules again over the two rivers and a very exhausted Battalion finally arrived and harboured again in "the Orchard" just south of Buthidaung. We had a rest that night, but the following day were ordered to stand by to move south, between the Mayu Range and the Mayu River. All stores and ammunition were loaded into Sampans to be carried south down stream. This was done but at midnight the order was countermanded and all stores were to be unloaded immediately. This was also done and the following day the Battalion moved south again down the Kingdaung road to a position near Taungmaw just south of the Aungtha Chaung opposite Point 201. Again, everything had to be moved across the two rivers and it was remarkable how cheerful the Battalion remained despite this extremely hard and exhausting and seemingly unnecessary work. It was now that evacuations through sickness began to become really serious. This was almost invariably ascribed to malaria. It would be difficult to argue with the medical experts on this matter, but it seems certain that whatever was the cause of the sickness it was greatly aggravated by the quite unnecessary fatigue imposed on all ranks. Heat exhaustion and lack of sleep tend no doubt to lower the resistance to malaria. Very few reinforcements were arriving and the Battalion was now very much below strength. At Taungmaw we came under command of Brigadier Bull of 71 Brigade again, to the great satisfaction of all concerned.

The Battalion stayed in the Taungmaw area for some time engaged in active and long distance patrolling, but no contact was made with the enemy. Shells fell in the area on one occasion and once a Jap reconnaissance plane came over very low and was later brought down. Two long patrols of several days were taken out to the east by Lieuts. Griffin and Munroe but failed to make any contact with the enemy.

It was now decided that the monsoon line should run as far south and east as Kingdaung and 71 Brigade was ordered to withdraw. The 1st Lincolns were ordered to hold the Kingdaung area with a view to remaining there throughout the monsoon. The Battalion moved back by night and again crossed the rivers with all stores, ammunition and mules. It was perhaps just as well that we did not know at that time that the Japanese were to get the whole lot except the mules in less than a month's time, early in May.

The next few days were spent in reconnoitring the new positions and making a start on arrangements for the monsoon. Luckily these did not get far and no very great amount of work was carried out. It was now decided to have a detached force east of the Mayu River consisting of the Lincolns and various small units. This was to be known as " Gates Force" but died at, or almost before birth, to be replaced by " Sinker Force" which had a slightly longer life and consisted of two Companies only, with orders to resist any enemy attack and to fight if necessary a rearguard action to Buthidaung. The rest of the Battalion moved off through Buthidaung to positions about two miles west of the town. The main enemy activity at this time was up the Mayu Range itself and between the river and the range. East of the river very little was seen of the enemy.

It was at this time that Lt. Colonel P. H. Gates was promoted to Brigadier to command 55 Brigade which was engaging the enemy south west of Buthidaung. Major Sinker handed over the two Companies at Kingdaung to Major Hoey—it now became " Hoey Force"—and assumed command of the 1st Lincolns.

CHAPTER IV.

WITHDRAWAL TO NHILA.

Battalion Headquarters was now situated at Dongyaung, about a mile south of the Buthi-daung-Maungdaw Road and the Battalion was scattered over a very large area.   Two Companies were east of the Mayu River—" B " Company, Major Hoey and " C " Company, Captain Homersham—in the Kingdaung area.   " D " Company, Major Hill, was in the hills just south of Buthidaung and "A" Company, Major Innes, with Battalion Headquarters, mortars, signallers and carriers were at Dongyaung.   The Battalion Administrative Area with Captain Sidwells and Lt. (Q.M.) Tancred was on the road by an iron bridge about a mile in rear of Battalion Headquarters.   One platoon under Lieut. Lord Saville was guarding a bridge over a chaung half-way between Buthidaung and Kingdaung.   A small detachment from " D " Company was gurading the ferry at Buthidaung.   The distance from Battalion Headquarters to Headquarters " Hoey force" was about twelve miles by road with one ferry crossing.

Evacuations through sickness, mostly malaria, were now very high and over a hundred a week was quite normal.   Reinforcements were arriving but not in sufficient numbers to keep pace with the evacuations.   The time had now come when the Battalion, except for a small nucleus, was more a collection of strange individuals than a cohesive unit.   The rapidity with which the new officers and men settled down and became " Lincolns" did them great credit and many who joined then remained with the Battalion till the end of the war.   Amongst them were Lieut West, later to become Adjutant, and C.S.M. Hutchinson, to become R.S.M.

The Jap threat and drive up the Mayu Range was intensifying and 55 Brigade were actively engaged to the south.   No serious attempt was made to attack " Hoey force" though they were subjected to occasional shelling to which they replied when possible with mortar fire. 36 Brigade now arrived on the scene and the North Staffordshire Regiment passed through us to do a flanking attack.   This, however, was cancelled and they returned the following day.

The carriers were most useful, especially for working with " Hoey force."   Rations had to be sent down daily and the Commanding Officer paid visits every few days.   As the road from Buthidaung to Kingdaung might be found to be held by the enemy any day their rations had to be escorted and a carrier was the safest vehicle in which to travel.   Major Hoey also made use of them to move about in his area, when the dust could be seen for miles, to mislead the Japs as to the strength of his force.

Jap air attack now became a bit more active and Buthidaung was bombed, and one of the valuable motor ferries was sunk.   The few remaining local inhabitants were the chief sufferers in this raid.

Strenuous patrolling was carried out, particularly to the west into the Mayu Range, south to contact 55 Brigade, and east from " Hoey force."   The Royal Navy who had a detachment and two motor craft at Buthidaung assisted in this down the Mayu River.

The enemy continued to infiltrate through the dense jungle at the Mayu Range and every night their red tracer could be seen which appeared to float across the sky and seemed to be a form of signalling and giving of direction.

Early on May 3rd " Tamil " was attacked on their position by the iron bridge on the road, telephone communication broke down and the track from Battalion Headquarters to the road was now open to enemy mortar and small arms fire, and could only be risked at full speed in a carrier.   We had been told that at all costs we must hold the mouth of the Kakybyet chaung which ran out from the Mayu Range from the west opposite the Headquarters position at Dongyaung.   Fighting patrols were frequently sent up this chaung and frequently clashed with the enemy when both sides suffered casualties.   Lieut. Page and C.S.M. Cressy did invaluable work in this chaung which was also kept under constant fire from the Battalion mortars. During one of the patrols one of our men was captured. He was taken back a short distance where his captors were just about to knock out his brains when they were stopped and he was given to understand by signs that he could go. He wasted no time over this and ran off down the chaung whilst the Japs took pot shots at him. He was hit in the arm but managed to disappear into the jungle and found his way back to the Battalion.

Once when a large force of Japs were reported to be collecting in the chaung we managed to get the guns on to them. This shoot was most unusual. The gunners' observation post was on a small hill above Battalion Headquarters, known the following year as " Spit." The guns that the Forward Observation Officer was directing through a relay of wirelesses were west of the tunnels and shooting short of but in almost direct line to the Observation Post. The gun fire was very accurate and at no time did any Jap get through the Kakybyet chaung during the time we were responsible for it.

Fever at this time was getting worse and field ambulances were working against time to get these cases and battle casualties away. The Commanding Officer had a bad attack of malaria at this time and for one day was forced to hand over command to Major Innes.

" Tamil " was still holding out though almost completely cut off and Major Sidwells and R.Q.M.S. Jessop had been wounded.

The Royal Air Force now became very active and made many successful strikes up and down the Mayu Range. One very successful strike, guided by smoke bombs from our mortars, was made on the enemy overlooking " Tamil."

Previous to the enemy break through, assembly areas had been reconnoitred and warning orders issued for a withdrawal.

The orders to withdraw were received on May 5th, to pass through 36 Brigade early on May 6th. These were issued to all concerned by whatever forms of communication that were still working. On the night of May 5th, 55 Brigade passed through " D " Company at Buthidaung.

We had been told that sufficient mules would be sent to Dongyaung before dawn on the 6th to lift our loads, other than those at " Tamil" which could not be saved. The mules did not turn up and Major Cotton galloped to 3 Brigade Headquarters, under whose command we had now been placed, for instructions. We were ordered to take what kit we could on our own mules, destroy the rest as far as possible and withdraw immediately. This was carried out and the Battalion assembled in the low hills just north of the Buthidaung road. " Hoey force" had made a clean getaway and arrived on time, having lost a carrier and an ambulance in the crossing of the river. The remnants of " Tamil " also managed to creep away before dawn and completely exhausted, joined up with us.

All motor transport was now withdrawn. Most of it was destroyed, but some, including our remaining carriers and station wagon, driven by Pte. Harris, under Captain Lawson, assisted by Sgt. Rushby, managed to make off to the north and finally reached Taung Bazaar from where they could move no further, and there were later dismantled and abandoned.

On reporting to Lt. Colonel Fawcett, acting Brigadier of 36 Brigade, the Battalion was ordered to take up a supporting position north of the Letwedet Chaung. At 1700 hours we were again ordered to withdraw and to make our way north and west across the Mayu Range by the Ngaukeydauk chaung and pass. Everyone by this time was very exhausted and on reaching the eastern end of the pass the Commanding Officer decided to halt for a meal and harbour for the night. Luckliy we had passed a forward supply dump of rations where we were allowed and in fact encouraged to take what we wanted. In the middle of the meal Brigadier Bull arrived. He was now commanding " Mayforce" and had very gallantly walked all the way across the Mayu Range to direct operations closer to the enemy. He gave orders that we were not to harbour but to push on and get across the pass as quickly as possible. We set out again in the dark and started through the jungle but before very long were forced to halt again after spending two or three hours before finally getting the mules across a deep chaung in pitch darkness. At first light the next morning we started again and began the long climb over the pass and finally reached Ponnezaik on the west of the Bawli Bazaar-Maungdaw road at about 1000 hours. We were met by Lieut. Latimer who informed us that tea and a hot meal were ready for us, which put new life into everyone.

General Lomax, who had now taken over 26 Division, met us here and we were ordered to move south again to take up a position in the area of the western tunnel on the Maungdaw-Buthidaung road. General Lomax also complimented the Battalion on their previous work and told us that he would try and give us at least one full night's rest. The Battalion moved to an area west of the tunnel in the afternoon, where a good night's rest was enjoyed. The following morning we started to take over from the Lancashire Fusiliers in the tunnel area and had taken over complete by the evening. This was a most tiring area to hold and " B " Company, the furthest away and the highest held Point 1401.

While we were in this position orders were received that 71 Brigade was to spend the monsoon at Nhila on the Teknaf peninsula about fifteen miles north and slightly west of Maungdaw. Major Innes and a small advanced party were sent off to do what they could in preparation for our arrival.

During our time at the tunnels we were not worried by the Japs except for some desultory shell fire. On May 11th, the Battalion made a slight withdrawal to a harbour in the foothills just south of Maungdaw and the following night moved north again. We picked up motor transport after a march of about eight miles and were lifted to Bawli Bazaar. Here we spent most of the day and in the late afternoon marched to Redwin Byin where we embarked on river steamers and barges and were lifted across the Naaf River and disembarked at Nhila, where we were met by Major Innes.

By this time the Battalion was very under strength and deficient in all stores and equipment. Those that were left were very tired. The strength of the Battalion on arrival at Nhila was about 350 out of our establishment of 830. The officers in Battalion Headquarters and Headquarters Company had dwindled to the Commanding Officer, Lt. Col. Sinker, Capt. Cotton, the Adjutant, Capt. Craig the Medical Officer and Captain Williams, the Padre. We were very lucky still to have four senior Company Commanders, "A" Company, Major Innes, " B " Company, Major Hoey, " C " Company, Captain Homersham, and " D " Company, Major Hill. Lieut. Tancred the Quartermaster though very ill, had managed to hang on as far as Bawli Bazaar where he had collapsed.

Our battle casualties had not been heavy and when we had met the enemy we had more than held our own. Three months living in the open—we had no mosquito nets, and mepacrine at this time was not always available and not taken very seriously—constant moves combined with long marches, the moving about of tons of stores and the preparation of new positions, took a very heavy toll in sickness. During the three months in the Arakan in 1943—Nhila is on the border and just in Bengal—we averaged three days between moves. We had, however, learnt two important lessons. The jungle had ceased to worry us, and though we had been thrown out by the Japs we felt that we now knew him and would be more than a match for him when we met again.

CHAPTER V.

NHILA.

Nhila is a small village on the banks of the Naaf River which at this point is nearly a mile wide. About two miles north on the other side, the Pruma Chaung, which leads to Bawli Bazaar, joins the Naaf. The river is very tidal with a very strong current and at times can be unpleasantly rough for small boats.

The land is cultivated with paddy near the village, which soon becomes jungle to the west, rising to a range of hills running north and south up to a height of about 900 feet. On the west of the range the country slopes down to the sea with a wide, flat, sandy beach stretching north and south as far as the eye can see ; in the north past Elephant Point to Cox's Bazaar, and in the south past Teknaf to the small island of Shodapur. The jungle was thick but made up here more of large trees than of bamboo and undergrowth and in places was quite beautiful. Nhila was in fact a most attractive place and as yet unspoilt.

The inhabitants, who were predominantly Maghs, were friendly and helpful though we never felt that we could trust them very far. During the four months we were in Nhila we always remained on good terms and had no trouble of any kind. Near the south end of the peninsula was the fishing village of Teknaf, separated from Maungdaw only by the Naaf River.

There were no roads and few tracks on the peninsula and later when we occupied Teknaf all movement was carried out by river. A track led across the centre range from Nhila to Matabangha, a very small village on the coast. This was later made passable for mules. Communications to the north were by boat to Tumbru Ghat which was road and river head. Local supplies at first were fairly plentiful and very welcome after three months' continual bully beef and biscuits and consisted mainly of fish, chickens, eggs and fruit. Later fresh meat was made available.

On the morning of May 14th a reconnaissance of the new area was carried out with Brigadier Bull. At first the Brigade was disposed with Headquarters and 1st Lincolns at Nhila. The 7/15th at Matabangha and the 9/15th well to the north at Tumbra Ghat.

The first positions to be held by the Lincolns were Nhila, Chaudipara, a village about a mile due south, and Monastery Hill on top of which was a Magh monastry inhabited by yellow robed monks.

These positions were changed many times during the next few months after many reconnaissances and discussions in which many senior officers took part.

On one unforgettable day, after Brigade Headquarters had moved back to Tumbru we were visited by the G.O.C. in C., General Sir George Gifford, the Corps Commander, Lt. General Slim, the Divisional Commander, Major General Lomax, and Brigadier Bull, accompanied by staff including the C.R.A. and the A.D.M.S. After the visit the positions were changed slightly—though we still held Chaudipara, over which the main battle was fought.

We were given to understand that despite our many good qualities in other directions our efforts at digging and camouflage were quite inadequate. This, on the whole, was true and we had a lot to learn and never at any time were our defensive positions comparable with those of the Japanese. The Battalion never actually became good diggers though they have been known to use bayonets and knives and forks to get some kind of cover when under heavy enemy fire. In operations in 1944 and 1945 we found few tactical positions in the Arakan that had not been previously occupied and dug over and usually managed to find our defences more or less ready for us.

The first four weeks of our stay in Nhila were taken up with the preparation of the defences and reorganising and refitting. We also had frequent visits and inspections, anti-malarial precautions were strictly enforced and the Battalion in general thoroughly smartened up. Reinforcements began to arrive and our own sick and wounded to come back and we were soon over strength. Shortly after arrival we started patrolling again and were responsible for the whole of the Teknaf peninsula south of Nhila. We also had a special hunting ground east of the river, an area immediately north of Maungdaw, known as Maungdaw North Island. A special guerilla Platoon was formed which at times had several commanders including Lieuts. Snelling, Page, Walker and Jenkins. Their job was to get across the river and harass the Japs and bring back useful information and, if possible, prisoners. The crossing of the Naaf River by night was always an arduous undertaking in sampans and we had several casualties by drowning and lost a good deal of equipment. We, however, gained the initiative and not once during our stay in Nhila did the Japs set foot on the Teknaf Peninsula. Sgt. Snelling and Pte. Neilus were well known members of the guerilla platoon and both in time received the M.M. Our first decoration actually came through at this time and we heard that Major Innes had been awarded the Military Cross.

Training was carried out in conjunction with the patrols and upkeep of defences and those that could be spared above a minimum strength were sent on leave mostly to Calcutta and Darjeeling. The fever incidence decreased and the health of the Battalion was comparatively good. Special attention was paid to shooting with all weapons at short ranges. By the middle of June we had settled down and the Battalion was disposed, mostly as a striking force, as follows :—

Battalion Headquarters and two Companies at Nhila, one Company at Chaudipara, and one Company at Teknaf, with a detached platoon on the west coast at Matabangha. The 7/15th was disposed with Headquarters on Monastery Hill and two Companies east of the river at Redwinbyn. "A" and "B" Companies of the Lincolns under Major Hoey, with Captain Munroe commanding "A" Company had originally gone over the river but had come back in order to keep the Battalion concentrated in the role of a striking force. The 9/15th and Brigade Headquarters were at Tumbra Ghat. 26 Division Headquarters were slightly further back at Taungbroo. 36 Brigade were in the Bawli Bazaar area and 4 Brigade at Cox's Bazaar. The Japanese held Maungdaw, the tunnels and at this time more or less shared the Ngaukeydauk pass.

The Battalion had to make quite a lot of use of the river and to employ the local sampans. We never became good sailors and we had many adventures, some tragic and some amusing. There was one motor boat known as the *Eureka* belonging to Brigade Headquarters which worked between Tumbra Ghat, Nhila and Teknaf, more often calling at Jackson's Jetty, just north of Teknaf, to keep out of sight of Maungdaw. At one time the Battalion was given an old lifeboat, of the push and pull lever type. A volunteer crew manned this but it proved to be too heavy to be of much value. On one occasion the Captain, a Corporal who possibly lived by the sea in Lincolnshire, thought he had found a good sheltered and concealed anchorage just north of Teknaf. This unfortunately turned out to be the corner of a flooded paddy field on the top of a spring tide. The boat was not floated again for a considerable time after much labour. We were also given four small punts with outboard motors. The idea was to anchor these by night in a line across the river at Chaudipara to prevent any enemy coming up. However, they were not big or stout enough to compete with the very strong tide and after a few trials this was given up.

Captain Cotton was now nearing the end of his turn as Adjutant. Captain Duval of the Mortar Platoon was chosen to understudy him and Lieut. Ryan to take over the mortars. Both these officers stayed in their new appointments till the end of the war.

Towards the end of June bashas had been built for accommodation, a new village had sprung up and the whole of the Battalion was under cover and quite comfortable. The monsoon had started and the rainfall was heavy and frequent and the country became waterlogged. Patrols were now troubled with leeches, but as with everything else we soon got used to these. There were many wild elephant in the jungle on the peninsula and we were lucky to have no encounters with them. A small patrol of the 9 15th had met one earlier on and shot at it with the result that two of the party were killed.

General Lomax now ordered a large scale raid to be made on Maungdaw with the object of further harassing the Japs, capturing a prisoner, destroying stores and getting information. Brigadier Bull came down and we spent several days in planning before taking the result up to the General, who approved. The force to take part consisted of one rifle Company, a platoon of Machine Guns from the Frontier Force, a section of Indian sappers, the Guerilla Platoon and a small Regimental Aid Post. " B " Company, under command of Major C. F. Hoey, was selected for the task.

The plan was fairly involved and depended almost entirely on tides. We had at our disposal one river steamer, eight large sampans capable of holding about thirty to forty men, the *Eureka* and numbers of small sampans. Directly above Maungdaw three chaungs joined the Naaf River : the Tat Chaung at Maungdaw separating the town from the North Island, the Kanyin Chaung running north of North Island, and the Pyinbyu Chaung about three miles north of this about opposite to Jackson's Jetty. We had working with us at this time a detachment of " V " force, an irregular force with British Officers using local inhabitants to get information and perform acts of sabotage. This party was asked unobtrusively to collect sufficient small sampans to lift a company at a point where the Tat Chaung met the Kanyin Chaung after turning north near Lettha, a mile or so north east of Maungdaw. They were also asked to find out and answer various definite questions as regards the tide in the three chaungs north of Maungdaw at various selected points.

The plan in general was to form two bridgeheads, most of the guerilla platoon just north of the bridge leading across the Tat Chaung from Maungdaw, the remainder with the machine guns platoon at the north end of North Island. While these were being established " B " Company was to move in large sampans down the Naaf, up the Pyinbyu Chaung, to disembark and after a short march re-embark in small sampans and move to Lettha where they would lie up for a whole day and night. Here they were to watch for Japs and send out small reconnaissance patrols before making their final plan for the assault on Maungdaw. The Sappers and Miners were to go with " B " Company for demolition purposes and for the setting of booby traps.

Large sampans could not move against the tide so a very careful time-table had to be worked out in order to catch the correct tide at the correct time at the correct place. For instance, the bridge-head parties leaving from Jackson's Jetty had to leave at the very end of the ebb tide to float down the Naaf whilst going across, just in time to catch the incoming tide at the mouth of the Kanyin Chaung to take them up to the landing place on North Island.

The raiding party which was to leave from Nhila were to be towed down by river steamer and dropped at the mouth of the northernmost chaung with a rising tide to carry them up. All movement on the river had, of course, to be carried out by night.

The preparations and briefing for the raid took several days but everything was ready and a start was made as planned on July 5th. The parties for the bridge heads had been sent off to Jackson's Jetty ostensibly to form a camp the day before, together with advanced Battalion Headquarters which was to be set up in the forest bungalow just south of the jetty. Troops were embarked in the evening and two sampans were lashed alongside the steamer and two were to be towed. Just before dark the steamer set off, the two sampans were taken in tow and the party set off upstream towards Tumbru Ghat, steaming in that direction until it was dark and then turning round. It was a rough night and pitch dark. Two men had been ordered to be sent over from Jackson's Jetty to the mouth of the Pyinbyu Chaung with a torch to flash at intervals northwards at the time that the steamer was scheduled to arrive. About five miles south of Nhila we had the first of many setbacks. With very little warning one of the sampans in tow containing the sappers and miners and all their stores got out of control and capsized. Most of the men were fortunately saved but all the stores were lost. C.S.M. Hutchinson, of " B " Company did some very gallant and successful rescue work. The remaining sampan was now lashed alongside and we steamed on, still having time to reach the Chaung according to plan. Presently we picked up the flash light, the steamer anchored close inshore and the three sampans were cast off. The steamer had unfortunately gone too close and was stuck fast. Every effort was made to get clear with no success. At dawn we were able to see that the situation was still worse than we thought. The light had been flashed from a small inlet which had been mistaken for the Chaung in the intense darkness and rain, and two of " B " Company's sampans were still in the Naaf river making great efforts to get into the northern chaung. The third was not in sight. We signalled across to advanced Headquarters with a flash light calling urgently the *Eureka*, and after great difficulty managed to get the message through and the motor boat came across. At this time we could see a sampan coming upstream on the west side of the river with troops on board and this could only be the missing " B " Company boat. The *Eureka* went off and took it in tow to join the rest of " B " Company, now well up the Pyinbyu Chaung. The sampan had damaged her rudder when being cast off, had been quite unmanageable in the strong tide and floated down the Naaf past Maungdaw during the night and returned again with the flood tide. Later with the help of the *Eureka* it was found possible to get the steamer afloat and she returned to Nhila. We all felt rather depressed at this time as we thought that all hope of surprising the enemy must now have been lost.

We had been given some No. 18 wireless sets for the raid but wireless silence had been ordered until " B " Company actually got into Maungdaw. Things now took a turn for the better and everything went according to plan. During the whole of the operation the wireless only worked once when we got a message to the effect that " B " Company was in Maungdaw. Divisional Headquarters actually got the first news of this, reported by a Hurricane pilot.

As there was no news on the wireless the Commanding Officer decided to take the *Eureka* across to the bridgehead on North Island. Here he met Lieut. Snelling commanding the guerillas, Captain Battram the Medical Officer and the Machine Gun Officer. A message came through from Major Hoey to the effect that he intended to start to withdraw at dusk and to pass through the bridgeheads as planned. The original plan was to return in the same way in the large sampans but the Commanding Officer decided to modify this and ferry the troops direct from North Island in the *Eureka* to the steamer, and ordered the steamer to move south opposite the entrance to Kanyin Chaung. The ferrying was carried out later in three trips and a final and fourth trip was made with the two sampans lashed alongside containing the two bridgehead parties. After a very rough trip these were cast off at Teknaf and the *Eureka* joined the steamer and sailed for Nhila. There was one wounded man on board with a very serious head wound and Captain Battram decided to go straight on to Tumbru with him in the *Eureka* where there was a chance that the surgical team might save his life. Despite every effort this was unsuccessful.

We now learnt all about the raid which in the end had actually completely surprised the enemy. Maungdaw had been held for the day, the Japs had suffered fairly heavy casualties—twenty had been killed—a lot of stores had been taken and a post bag containing Jap mail had been captured. Our own casualties were one killed and two wounded. The Company also brought back an enemy light machine gun. Morale was very high and the Battalion received congratulations from the C. in C. India, the G.O.C. in C. Eastern Command, the Corps Commander and the Divisional Commander. Major Hoey was awarded the Military Cross.

The following diary of events has been compiled by Captain North who commanded one of the platoons of " B " Company.

REPORT ON OPERATION " OTTER." (Chronological Order of Events).

Date.	Time.	Climatic Conditions.	Events.
10 July '43	1830 hrs.	Drizzle	" B " Company, 1 Lincolns, and section of Sappers embarked and loaded sampans.
	2000 hrs.	Drizzle. No moon.	Finished attaching sampans to river steamers by rope and force sailed up Naaf River towards Tumbru Ghat.
	2100 hrs.	,,	Steamer turns and sails down river towards Maungdaw.

OPERATION OTTER
PHASE I AND II

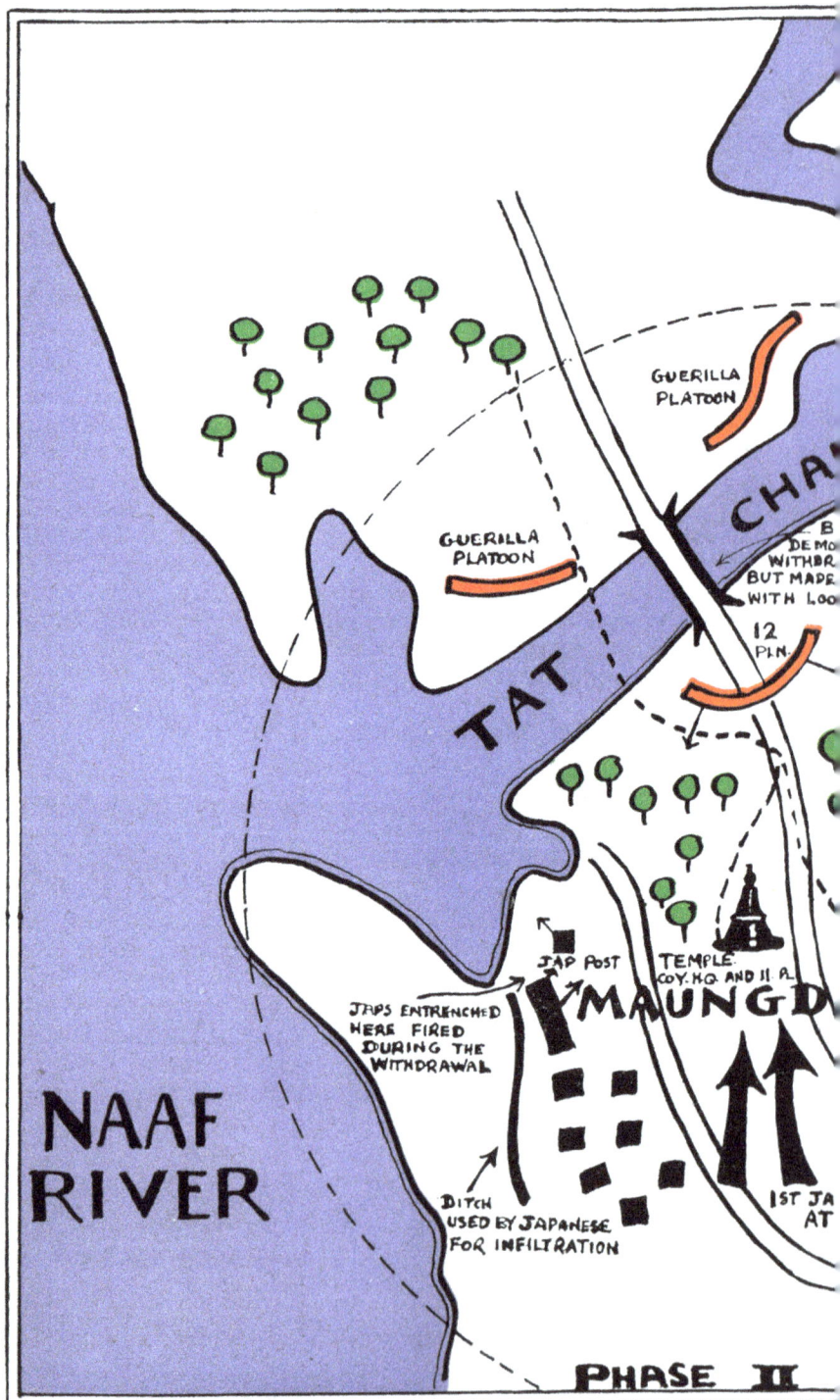

GUERILLA
PLATOON

CHA

GUERILLA
PLATOON

B
DE MOI
WITHDR
BUT MADE
WITH LOO

TAT

12
PLN

JAP POST

TEMPLE
COY. HQ AND II P.

JAPS ENTRENCHED
HERE FIRED
DURING THE
WITHDRAWAL

MAUNGD

NAAF
RIVER

DITCH
USED BY JAPANESE
FOR INFILTRATION

1ST JA
AT

PHASE II

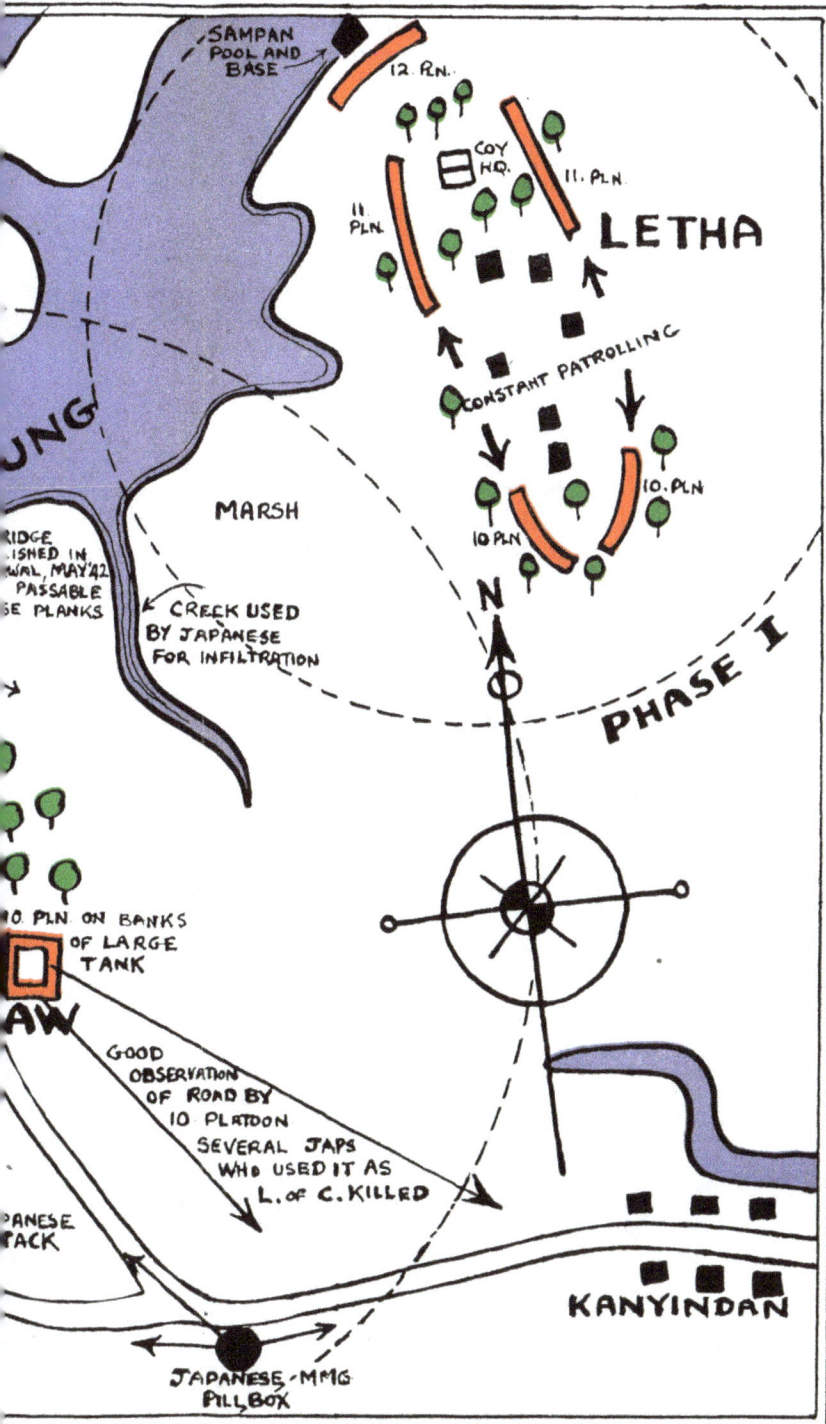

SCALE — 1 INCH = 250 YDS.

SAMPAN POOL AND BASE

12. PLN.

COY HQ.

11. PLN.

11. PLN.

LETHA

CONSTANT PATROLLING

10. PLN

MARSH

10 PLN

N

RIDGE
...ISHED IN
...WAL, MAY'42
PASSABLE
...E PLANKS

CREEK USED BY JAPANESE FOR INFILTRATION

PHASE I

10. PLN ON BANKS OF LARGE TANK

...AW

GOOD OBSERVATION OF ROAD BY 10 PLATOON SEVERAL JAPS WHO USED IT AS L. of C. KILLED

...PANESE
...ACK

KANYINDAN

JAPANESE MMG PILLBOX

Date.	Time.	Climatic Conditions.	Events.
10 July ,'43	2230 hrs.		Sampan with Sapper Section and demolition apparatus capsizes. C.S.M. Hutchinson saves life of native oarsman. Two Sappers missing. Later found intact. Sapper section written off.
	2359 hrs.	Raining hard Pitch black.	River steamer stops—Hoey force prepares to cast off. Chaung, up which force is to move in sampans, supposed to be opposite river steamer.
11 July, '43	0030 hrs.	,,	Force casts off and rows towards guide showing light at mouth of Chaung.
	0115 hrs.	Drizzle	Reach Chaung mouth—cannot contact guide but proceed up Chaung. Tide is rapidly going out.
	0130 hrs.	,,	Sampans touch bottom. Major Hoey realises that force has proceeded down wrong Chaung.
	0130 hrs. to 0230 hrs.	,,	Attempt to turn sampans—reach Naaf River and find right Chaung. Tide has receded too fast and bulk of sampans are stuck fast on mud. River steamer stands by to help and gets stuck on mud bank. Force settled down resignedly to wait for morning and high tide. Tide right out—unfor-
	Dawn	Stopped raining but cloudy.	gettable sight. All craft, including river steamer seemingly deposited in the middle of a paddy field. There is talk of cancelling operation as objective is not very far off (approx. 3 miles) and as news travels fast—element of surprise would now have been lost. Major C. Hoey decides to carry on as planned.
	1000 hrs.	No rain.	Tide has risen and force proceeds up correct Chaung (which was only 100 yards South of Chaung that had caused so much trouble).
	1600 hrs.	Still no rain.	Hoey Force quite happy—a bit hungry, would appreciate a mug of " char." Reach first objective near village of Habispara and are met by " V " Force agent, Capt. Guinsberg. Due to monsoons the village resembles Venice and movement can only be achieved by sampan.
	1600 hrs. to 1700 hrs.		Force tranships with stores from large sampans to smaller ones leaving rear party of two men with large sampans.
	1800 hrs.	Commenced to rain.	Reach Habispara school house (tumbledown build- ing with roof that leaks). Eat meal—brew up tea— receive first alarm of approaching Jap patrol. Force lies very low till alarm has passed over.
12 July, '43	0100 hrs.	Drizzle.	Force woken up—prepare to move to final position prior to objective, the village of Letha. Move is on foot, distance approximately three miles, difficult country, many Chaungs to be waded through, some chest deep. Capt. Guinsberg had made reconnais- ance of route before, now acting as guide.
	0445 hrs.	Rain stopped.	Arrived at Letha.

DESCRIPTION OF VILLAGE.

Three hundred yards long and between fifty and hundred yards wide—heavily wooded. Native

Date.	Time.	Climatic Conditions.	Events.
			population approximately one hundred. Observation from village very good. Main Maungdaw-Buthidaung Road easily observed with naked eye. Over paddy fields to Kanyindan (village on road). Maungdaw and bridge joining North to South islands (over Tat Chaung) also easily visible. Ground between Letha and Maungdaw very swampy, full of Chaungs, could only be crossed at low tide on foot ; distance approximately one mile. Best form of movement by boat.
12 July, '43	0500 hrs.	Rain stopped.	Hoey Force whilst still quite dark garrisons Letha, not so much with a view of defence but to prevent inhabitants leaving village and informing Japs. All inhabitants very friendly, well stocked with food which had been looted from Supply Depots when Army had withdrawn in May. Natives very friendly, Headman particularly. Sold us looted tin food at fantastic prices. Force however was glad to have it. (For dispositions see Sketch B).
	0500 hrs.	Sunny.	1. Not disturbed.
			2. Force remained very quiet observing.
			3. Japs seen moving on Maungdaw-Buthidaung Road.
			4. Also suspected Japs on bridge over Tat Chaung.
			5. Noise of North Staffs. operation heard. Jap artillery used.
			6. Several engineering materials salvaged. These were sent back to Habibpara and the large sampans.
			7. Major C. Hoey called conference at 1800 hours. Result of conference—
			(*a*) Two reconnaissance patrols to go out at 2000 hours (four hour duration).
			(*b*) Strength, one officer and one man.
			(*c*) *General object :* Reconnaissance of Kanyindan and Maungdaw in order to decide which would be more worth raiding.
			(*d*) Patrols to be found by 10 and 11 Platoons led by respective Officers Commanding.
	2000 hrs. to 2330 hrs.		10 Platoon patrol (responsible for Kanyindan) fails to go out owing to shot fired by sentry in error—might have put Japs in Kanyindan area on their guard.
			11 Platoon patrol sets out. Maungdaw reached by boat without incident. Jap (?) sentries seen by bridge over Tat Chaung, otherwise village seemed deserted.
	2000 hrs. to 2330 hrs.	No rain. Very dark.	What were previously believed to be fortifications found to be timber yard. Jap post although not seen located by noise. Patrol returns and reports. Major C. Hoey decides to raid Maundgaw at dawn.

Date.	Time.	Climatic Conditions.	Events.
13 July, '43	0430 hrs.		S.T. from Letha.
	0530 hrs.	Rain.	Arrival at bridge by Tat Chaung. Sampans used to move force. No incidents except during actual move by boat, it rained so hard that one boat filled up and sank—no casualties, and boat was salvaged and put afloat again.
	0530 hrs. to 0830 hrs.	Rain stopped.	Force deployed for sweep through village. 10 and 11 Platoons with Company Headquarters to do sweep, 12 Platoon to remain at bridge. Surprised Jap post during sweep, consisting of one officer and nine men—Jap sentry fired on 10 Platoon who rushed post killing most of occupants. Those who ran away killed by 11 Platoon except one who although believed wounded got away. No prisoners taken but *identifications* found.
	0830 hrs.		Second sweep. Alarm had by now been raised and machine guns at cross roads opened up on force, wounding one man and knocking Major Hoey's crown off his shoulder. Officer Commanding " B " Company disposes his force for expected Jap attack. (See Sketch C).
	0900 hrs. to 1100 hrs.	Sunny day.	Continuous firing by Japs including mortars. Casualty effectively removed and taken to firm base at Kappagaung where Medical Section attended to him, Stretcher bearers of Hoey Force acting magnificently despite heavy small arms fire.
	1130 hrs.		Jap attack by approximately Company strength materialises. Object of attack to overrun Temple where Company Headquarters and 11 Platoon is entrenched. Attack is beaten back easily with heavy casualties inflicted on Japs. 10 Platoon on left meanwhile received the brunt of Jap covering fire and suffered one casualty (shot through head). Casualty was evacuated but died later at Tumbru Ghat Hospital
	1200 hrs. to 1600 hrs.		Artillery open up. Japs give up idea of direct assault and start infiltration tactics to cut Hoey Force in two. Several casualties believed inflicted on Japs but enemy successful on West flank.
	1600 hrs.		Patrol commanded by Pte. Paley sent out to discover extent of infiltration. Extensive infiltration reported but one Jap (believed to be W.O. by badges of rank) was personally stalked by Pte. Paley and killed. .
	1700 hrs.		Report from 12 Platoon at bridge that strong force of Japs starting to infiltrate on East flank using Chaungs.
	1730 hrs.		Major C. Hoey decided to withdraw 10 and 11 Platoons to be covered over Tat Chaung by 12 Platoon. Order of withdrawal. 10 Platoon—Company Headquarters covered by 11 Platoon, 11 Platoon covered by 12 Platoon when bridge is reached.

Date.	Time.	*Climatic Conditions.*	*Events.*
13 July, '43	1800 hrs.		Withdrawal completed without incident despite Japs having appreciated situation and had laid down very heavy fire along our route. Jap infantry also advancing as own troops withdraw. 12 Platoon as rearguard at bridge acted magnificently despite their precarious position. As bridge over Tat Chaung was under fire it could not be used. Sampans were employed and the native oarsmen acted with a courage very seldom shown by the Arakanese.
	1800 hrs.	Dry.	*Most surprising incident.*
			Once having crossed the Tat Chaung the wood was still not completely out of the fire. Before the force could reach cover of any sort paddy fields extending 200 yards approximately had to be crossed. Although the Guerilla Platoon was in position, in order to prevent enemy from crossing the river in pursuit, there was nothing to prevent the Japs who had already reached the South bank to open up with everything they had. The paddy field crossing was to be done in one concentrated rush (very difficult as the water was up to the knees). During the "mad rush" for cover the enemy opened up with everything, yet no casualties were suffered.
	1830 hrs.		Kappagaung was reached where Lt. Col. C. A. C. Sinker, D.S.O., met the force and organised its return to Nhila by river steamer.

TOTAL CASUALTIES IN OPERATION.

ENEMY.   Approx. 50 (including 22, killed).   OWN TROOPS : 1 killed, 2 wounded.

While at Nhila we first heard about the Jiffs, Indian soldiers who had joined the enemy. There were many rumours about this force and at one time thousands were reported to be collecting near Maungdaw with a view to invading Teknaf Peninsula. Nothing ever came of this though extra precautions were taken and special arm-bands were worn by Indian patrols likely to come into contact with British troops. Supplies at Nhila were always good and this was due largely to the Brigade Supply Officer, Captain Sewar Singh, who was a great friend of the Battalion and will always be remembered by those who served in the Arakan.

71 Brigade was now changed and the 1/18th Garhwal Rifles and the 5/1st Punjab Regiment relieved the 7th and 9th 15th Punjab Regiments.

General Christison assumed command of 15 Corps and General Slim of the 14th Army. The Battalion was relieved at the end of August with orders to march back to Doharazzi and there entrain for Chittagong, where we moved into a basha built camp later to become known as " Lincoln lines."

In their inimitable way the soldiers had adopted four small orphans, two little boys and two little girls whilst in the Arakan. These arrived safely back in Chittagong and were more or less taken officially on the strength. The two little girls were sent to a missionary school in Central India from which they immediately ran away and by methods known only to themselves arrived back in Chittagong in no way abashed. They were finally adopted by a very kind lady in Chittagong. The men subscribed Rs. 1400 for these children, and Tuppence and Whimpey, the two little boys, now aged about ten and nine, have been with the Battalion ever since, varying in rank from C.S.M. to Pte. according to their behaviour. At Chittagong we were able to send large parties off on leave and for about a month had a comparatively restful time. In November we were issued with about 300 live duck for our Christmas dinner. With very careful attention and a close guard, most of these survived until Christmas morning.

Everyone enjoyed the Christmas and on Boxing Day the Battalion gave a concert which was attended by General Lomax, Brigadier Bull and Lt. Colonel Cotterill-Hill, the G.I.

When most people were in bed the fire alarm went and the night was made hideous by the explosions of grenades and the crack of bullets. The signallers had set fire to two of their bashas which were completely destroyed with all their stores. This proved a very expensive night for the Regimental funds.

After Christmas we started to get down to really serious and intensive training and early in the new year moved out to a camp in the jungle at Barabakund about twenty miles north-west of Chittagong. The whole Battalion went to camp with Brigade Headquarters at Sitakund about five miles north of Battalion Headquarters.

CHAPTER VI.

RETURN TO THE ARAKAN AND ACTION AT POINT 315.

The Battalion worked really hard at Barabakund in all forms of training, night operations being particularly stressed. We had now been issued with new No. 48 wireless sets and were becoming very wireless minded. While in Barabakund we used no telephone by order of the Divisional Commander and thus began to place great reliance on wireless. Companies were well dispersed and this apart from runners was the only form of communication.

Towards the end of January Brigadier R. C. Cotterill-Hill, M.C., from Divisional Headquarters took over 71 Brigade from Brigadier Bull who left to take up the appointment of Director of Recruiting. He spent his last night with the Battalion with which he had been connected since 1936. Later he received the D.S.O. for his gallant and distinguished services in The Arakan.

We had just completed a strenuous two-day exercise in the jungle, during which Major Hill, who had recently been awarded the M.C., fell down a steep khud and seriously hurt his back, when the Division was again ordered south, back to the Arakan.

The Japanese under command of Colonel Tanabasha had staged a large scale flanking attack and had completely cut off 7th Indian Division and reached the outskirts of Bawli Bazaar. They now held the two roads over the Mayu Range at Ngakyedauk and the Tunnels. 71 Brigade was the first to move and proceeded by train through Chittagong to Dohazari and then by motor transport to Bawli Bazaar. The Battalion arrived at Bawli on the night of February 7th. The next morning some necessary stores were issued and later in the day " B " Company, followed by "A" Company, marched over the Goppe Pass with mule transport. The rest of the Battalion moved over the next morning, now under command of Brigadier Lowther of 4 Brigade. The Battalion was now on an all A.T. basis and needed about 350 mules to move complete. This could of course be largely cut down if we left bedding rolls and a greater part of first line ammunition behind. After a fairly stiff climb over the Pass the Battalion reached Goppe Bazaar and after a reconnaissance went into "harbour." Jap air was fairly active and Bawli Bazaar was raided. We stayed in Goppe for a day or two with the exception of "A" Company who were sent down to take Taung Bazaar. This was done without opposition. While at Goppe we had our first experience of being rationed by air. Signal fires were lit and Dakotas came over by night and unloaded tons of supplies. With the Japs in the vicinity, with the necessary fires and the noise we were glad when this was over. The Indian troops with us were rather surprised, but came to the conclusion that it must be a sahibs' " burra din." We unfortunately suffered two casualties from the dropping, one follower being killed by a bale of compressed hay and one having his arm broken. Supply by air, however, had proved and was to prove absolutely invaluable and 7 Division could never have held out in the Sinzweya "box" without it.

The Battalion now began to work its way south just east of the Mayu Range. Lincolns were the leading troops. The advance was necessarily a bit slow as the whole Division had to get across the Goppe Pass and supplies had to be built up and could only be moved by mule or air. On the 12th the Battalion arrived at Prinkaung with a battery of 3.7 howitzers under command. In the afternoon we advanced about six miles with the battery to get within gun-fire range of the enemy positions overlooking 7 Division and did about an hour's shoot. This was entirely from the map so the results were not known, but it must have shown the enemy that they were now in danger of being outflanked themselves by 26 Division. On the following night the Battalion was ordered to try and get through the jungle and join up with 7 Division. We set off with all our mules in the dark and fortunately struck the enemy early. At the first outbreak of firing all the mules stampeded, luckily in fairly open and flat country. Any further advance that night was impossible and the Battalion spent the next day collecting mules and kit. We had our first casualties and Lieut. Bustard, the leading Platoon Commander, was killed. We again moved south to Badana West. During this time we were carrying out very active patrolling but seeing very little of the enemy. At Badana we got orders by telephone to make a raid through the Japanese lines and to attack their positions on Point 315 overlooking the " Sinzweya Box." Information about the enemy was practically nil and of our own troops very vague. Two Companies, lightly equipped, with as much of Headquarters Company as was considered necessary, were to carry out this attack. We had with us a 22 wireless set for communication to Brigade.

A broad valley, which had been mainly paddy, about half a mile wide, ran south from Prinkaung past Badana practically to the Ngaukeydauk Chaung. This narrowed a bit about half-way when the Laung Chaung flowed across from west to east and this was an area of very thick scrub. On the west was the thick jungle rising up to the Mayu Range and on the east thick jungle again, covering hills about 200 to 300 feet high. The nearest known enemy position was in the jungle on the west, just south of the Laung Chaung. Moonrise was just after midnight and there was usually a ground mist which lasted until sunrise.

The Commanding Officer selected " B " Company, Major Hoey, and " D " Company, Captain Christison, as the rifle Companies. A small Battalion Headquarters was taken of the Commanding Officer, Capt. Duval, the Adjutant and Capt. Cheer, Signal Officer with a 22 set and two 48 sets. Headquarters Company detachment consisted of the Pioneer Platoon, two detachments under Lieut. Ryan and a Regimental Aid Post with Captain Battram and Major Pearson, the Medical Officer and Padre. Mules were reduced to a minimum of eight for the mortars and two for the 22 set. Equipment was light, a day's rations and cape being carried on the haversack. "A" Company, now under command of Major Innes again, were slightly south of Badana and were ordered to carry out constant patrolling of the Laung Chaung area until we were due to arrive as this was the main "snag" on our route. " D " Company and the Pioneer Platoon were sent off slightly in advance to find a track through the jungle at the Laung Chaung and to prepare a crossing if necessary for the mules. The banks of some of the chaungs were often perpendicular and very deep. No further information of the enemy was obtainable beyond the fact that he held Point 315 and his strength was unknown. The party set off at moonrise and moved in file down the centre of the valley in absolute silence. There was a thick ground mist which effectively hid us from view but made more difficult the keeping of direction. The ground was covered in rough, long grass, which hid the bunds, about one to two feet high, which had been used when the ground was under cultivation. In time we made contact with " D " Company who had so far failed to find a way through the jungle which turned out to be even thicker than expected. There was no alternative but to force and cut our way through, which we did, making as little noise as possible. After about an hour's hard work we came out the other side to find ourselves right on the western edge of the valley very near the known enemy position. The column turned sharp left and got past without being noticed and continued to advance down the centre of the valley which was now open again. The Japanese sentries must have been even less alert than usual as it was quite impossible to move in complete silence. " D " Company was now leading, followed by Headquarters and " B " Company. One of the mules started to bray which upset us but must have been quite a common sound as there were no doubt many loose mules wandering about the country at this time. Presently we came to a landmark and saw a small hill looming up on the left and we edged off to the right. This hill was later known as "Wings." The enemy may nor may not have been there when we passed. They certainly were later in the day. It was now that we first heard the Japs in the hills to the west and they were calling to each other and had now started to light some fires. We also heard some Urdu so we supposed that there were Jiffs amongst them. We came to a scrubby area nearly opposite Point 315 and reached the place which had been occupied by 7 Division Administrative Headquarters. In the dim and rather ghostly light this looked like a sleeping camp but on closer inspection it was obvious that it had been overrun and the unburied bodies of men and mules gave off a foul stench. The column was halted and the Commanding Officer with his orderly, Pte. Wilkinson, who was killed later in the morning, took a section from " D " Company and moved off to the right to reconnoitre a place to form up before attacking the hill. We had only gone about 200 yards when the Japs spotted us and opened fire with machine guns.

Hurrying back the Commanding Officer found the Company Commanders, and as " B " Company was concentrated and ready, ordered Major Hoey to take Point 315. Lieutenant Ryan got his mortars into action in a few minutes and the Commanding Officer told Major Hoey that he would follow up with " D " Company as soon as they could be collected. Charles Hoey dashed off, followed by his Company. The mortars shot well, the second bomb landing in a bunch of Japs who were seen no more, but they could not go on for long for fear of hitting " B " Company, who could not now be seen but only heard in the jungle going up the hill encouraged all the time by the voice of their Company Commander.

" D " Company were now ready and we followed up " B " Company with the Adjutant using the Pioneer Platoon as a rear party, keeping things safe behind. The advance gradually slowed down and Charles Hoey's voice could no longer be heard. He had reached his objective and had fallen at the top of the hill.

The Japs had been completely surprised and for a short time " B " Company had had their own way with bayonets, tommy guns and grenades. They found many of the enemy still rolled up in their blankets. The wounded now began to trickle down and the Regimental Aid Post was opened at the foot of the hill in a dried up chaung. The Japs were now shouting to each other but had recovered from their initial surprise. We held most of the hill but as usual it was well covered by fire from neighbouring hills. " D " Company were still making gallant efforts to get to the top but casualties were mounting rapidly and the Commanding Officer decided that no more could be done without support. He got back to the 22 set on the side of the hill, which was luckily working well and spoke to the Brigadier. He told him that he was going to withdraw to the broken and scrubby ground at the foot of the hill and reorganise. This was carried out and the battle died down for a time. Two tanks were suddenly seen approaching and not knowing that we had any east of the Mayu Range it was thought at first that they were enemy, but they turned out to be ours and we were able to make contact. Captain Duval was sent in one into the "box" with an account of the action and a request that we might be assisted with our wounded of whom we had about thirty-five. These had been a great source of anxiety and it now seems quite certain that had we had to leave them to the enemy they would have been massacred. The Adjutant got into the "box" safely, engaging some Jap anti-tank guns on the way and saw General Messervy who agreed to send out some carriers with the tanks to evacuate our wounded. He also agreed to let us have some tanks to assist in our withdrawal northwards which the Brigadier had now ordered.

The tanks also brought out some rations and water. In due course all the wounded were safely evacuated into the "box". We learnt later that it was in this area that the Japs had captured one of our Field Ambulances and had in cold blood murdered all the doctors and patients.

Captain Christison had by this time been wounded twice in the leg and neck but asked to be allowed to stay with his Company.

We were in a fairly strong position and the Japs seemed to have had enough so after we had brewed a very welcome

Evacuating wounded by mules after the battle of Point 315.

cup of tea we started off on our return journey at about 1600 hours. The route back was to be much the same, only keeping to the east side of the valley which seemed more likely to be free of enemy. The order of march was " D " Company, Headquarters and " B " Company, and we had two tanks in support. We got clear of the thick country and moved into the open, " D " Company in error moving west of " Wings." We could now see that most of the grass in the valley had been burnt down during the day and some was still burning. Very soon " D " Company came under heavy fire from the north end of " Wings" and at the same time long-range machine gun fire was opened from the hills to the west. There was also considerable mortar fire. The tanks took on what targets they could but we could not communicate with them and " D " Company, after a gallant charge by one Platoon were unable to get any further and were ordered back by wireless and at the same time " B " Company was ordered to continue the advance east of " Wings." The bursting of mortar bombs and the 75 m.m. gunfire from the tanks had proved too much for the mules, who now bolted with all their kit. " B " Company continued to advance unopposed and " D " Company was collecting ready to follow on. It was now getting dusk and the tanks withdrew. It was found that several of " D " Company's wounded were still lying out in the open and the Padre took a party of stretcher bearers and succeeded in bringing them in under fire. The Commanding Officer tried to check " B " Company by wireless but could not get in touch. They had, in fact, snapped the aerial of their wireless when moving through some jungle. It was now getting quite dark and we moved into the jungle on the right with the idea of following a track to the north which was marked on the map.

During the day "A" and " C " Companies had been moved slightly south, "A" Company being ordered to get into position on the east of the valley near the Laung Chaung to assist, if possible, in the withdrawal.

The track we were following soon petered out—it had probably been overgrown and the party halted and rested while we reconnoitred for a place to harbour till daybreak or possibly till moonrise. A suitable place on a hill was found after a time and we moved again and finally settled down till just before dawn.

When the moon came up the Commanding Officer collected three of the escort section and set out to try to find the track. After a time, thinking that he had found the way, he returned to the hill and was very lucky not to be met with a shower of grenades which the Adjutant had collected in his absence, as he had not warned everyone of his departure.

Just before dawn we moved off again off the hill where we might have been exposed to view. The track which had been found the previous night proved to be of no use and the Adjutant and a few men now went off on a short reconnaissance. They spotted some enemy to the west but could find no track. The Commanding Officer decided that the only thing to do was to cut a way through the jungle on a compass bearing making for "A" Company. We did this and continued until well into the afternoon when we struck the Laung Chaung about one hundred yards south of "A" Company. The wounded had been splendid and uncomplaining throughout though they must at time have been in great pain. C.S.M. Woods of " D " Company was one of the worst cases and later had to have both legs amputated. Lieut. Heaton who had taken over from Captain Christison was missing and known to be wounded or killed, and Lieut. Martin now commanded " D " Company. We continued the withdrawal together with "A" Company and joined up with " C " Company at Yinyinbang. " B " Company under Captain Neville had arrived earlier in the day, having followed the route of the previous night.

We had lost many old friends in this action but we had inflicted heavy losses on the enemy. His flanking thrust had now lost all its sting and the remnants of his force started to straggle back. The unexpected attack on his flank and rear on Point 315 no doubt did much to hasten his defeat. Major Charles Hoey, M.C., was posthumously awarded the Victoria Cross.

It was now decided to give the Battalion a short rest and after a night at Badana we marched back to Goppe Bazaar, arriving on February 18th and rejoined 71 Brigade under command of Brigadier Cotterill-Hill.

The Garhwals and Punjabis had also been in action with other Brigades and they too rejoined and 71 Brigade was again complete.

MAJOR C. F. HOEY, V.C., M.C.

EXTRACT FROM THE *London Gazette*, 16TH MAY, 1944.

The King has been graciously pleased to approve the posthumous award of the VICTORIA CROSS to :—

Captain (temporary Major) CHARLES FERGUSON HOEY, M.C., The Lincolnshire Regiment.

In Burma, on 16th February, 1944, Major Hoey's Company formed part of a force which was ordered to capture a position at all costs.

After a night march through enemy held territory, the force was met at the foot of the position by heavy machine-gun fire.

Major Hoey personally led his Company under heavy machine-gun and rifle fire right up to the objective. Although wounded at least twice in the leg and head he seized a Bren gun from one of his men and firing from the hip, led his Company on to the objective. In spite of his wounds the Company had difficulty in keeping up with him, and Major Hoey reached the enemy strong post first where he killed all the occupants before being mortally wounded.

Major Hoey's outstanding gallantry and leadership, his total disregard to personal safety and his grim determination to reach the objective resulted in the capture of this vital position.

TO MY SON, MAJOR C. F. HOEY, V.C.

I think that all is quiet where you are lying,
    The smoke and dust of battle long since gone.
Now little birds and shy small animals come freely
    About their daily life, while you sleep on—
When the first light of day touches the hilltop,
    Folding away the mist that evening laid
With careful hands to shield you from the darkness
    That you might rest there safe and unafraid,
One shining ray will light where you are lying,
    Spreading its radiance like a flag unfurled ;
A memory of the glory of your passing,
    And of the courage that you gave the world.

Duncan, B.C.   MARY HOEY.

The following messages were received when the award of Major Hoey's V.C. was announced :—

FROM THE ARMY COMMANDER.

" The Army Commander and all ranks of the 14th Army wish to convey to Officer Commanding 1 Lincolns their regret at the death of Major C. F. Hoey, M.C., to whom His Majesty the King has approved the posthumous award to the Victoria Cross. The gallantry and devotion to duty which won him this honour are testimony of the fine spirit of all ranks of the Battalion and the award of the Victoria Cross will be an inspiration not only to them but to the whole of the 14th Army."

FROM COMMANDERS 15 INDIAN CORPS AND 26 INDIAN DIVISION.

(1)   " Personal from Corps Commander to 1 Lincolns. With pride and sorrow I congratulate you all on the posthumous award of the V.C. to the late Major C. F. Hoey. I am glad that so fine an example of Lincoln valour has received the recognition it so richly deserved."

(2)   " My dear Sinker,

" You and your Lincolns must be very proud of Hoey's V.C. which was announced to-day. The award adds further laurels to the very fine Battalion which you command. Everyone in the Division shares your pride and is thankful that the award has been made. No V.C. was more worthily won."

Yours very sincerely,

CYRIL LOMAX,

At about this time the following special order of the Day was issued by The Commanding Officer down to platoons :—

SPECIAL ORDER OF THE DAY

BY

Lieutenant Colonel C. A. C. Sinker
Commanding 1st Battalion The Lincolnshire Regiment.

18th March, 1944.

To-day, March 18th, is the Anniversary of the first big action in which the 1st Battalion The Lincolnshire Regiment took part in the Arakan last year. This was the battle at Donbaik, which is some way south of Maungdaw. This attack was not completely successful, but the Battalion succeeded in reaching the objective with fairly heavy casualties, and only withdrew on orders from Higher Authority.

In no subsequent engagement since this date, in this Campaign or the last, have we failed in the attack to reach the objective, and we shall not fail in the future.

It must also be our determination and pride that we shall never, under any circumstances, move back from a position we have gained or been ordered to hold, unless we are given orders to do so.

Our reputation in India is probably second to none, but we have to fight and fight hard with untiring determination and a truly offensive spirit to maintain the reputation and to increase it.

All of us have seen our Regiment mentioned in the press recently and have felt proud that it should be so. This was earned by you. Some of you are new to the Battalion, but I hope that all of you feel that you are part of it from the moment you arrive, and that any success is due in some way, however great or small, to your personal behaviour. I hope that all of you, of whatever rank, will always be able to think and speak with pride of the Battalion in which you are now serving, when you go on leave, or in time to come, when the war is over and you go home. With this must be a feeling that it is your Battalion, made famous by your individual efforts.

This Battalion of the Lincolnshire Regiment was first formed 259 years ago, and was fighting in many places all over the world long before our enemies the Germans, Japanese and until lately, the Italians, existed or were thought of, as nations or Empires.

During this war, our fighting has been mainly confined to Burma. We are one of the few units, and the only British unit that has been sent back to fight a second campaign in the Arakan. We may well be proud of this. We can take it.

We have all seen something of the Japanese lately, and should all feel now that we are better men and soldiers than they. Furthermore, we are better equipped and better armed.

Let us go then into our future battles with confidence and courage, and with the knowledge that we are better than our enemies.

We have recently been set a very perfect example by Major Hoey. His grim determination, his supreme courage, and his willing self-sacrifice for his cause and Regiment, should be an inspiration to all of us.

If we all aim at this ideal, which is of the highest, nothing can go wrong, and we shall finish this campaign with great honour and distinction, and the firm knowledge that we have all taken our share and done our duty.

C. A. C. Sinker, Lieutenant Colonel

Commanding 1st Battalion the Lincolnshire Regiment.

CHAPTER VII.

ACTIONS IN THE WET VALLEY AND "SPIT AND POLISH."

The Battalion had a brief spell in Goppe and on February 23rd moved south again to Badana East.

Colonel Tanabasha's drive had been stopped and beaten back and the remnants of his force were now stragglers, for the most part very short of food and ammunition. It was now our job to try and round up small parties of the enemy by active patrolling and to stop them from rejoining their main forces further south. The Division gradually moved forward to the Maungdaw-Buthidaung road. The 81st West African Division was also moving south down the Kaladan Valley to the east. We took one or two prisoners at this time, but they were poor specimens and half starved. It was, however, very encouraging as Jap prisoners up to now had been extremely rare. Major Hill, Captain Lawson and Major Rayner, the Second in Command, rejoined us in Badana East. We occasionally augmented our rations here by killing a bullock and food was a great improvement on the previous year. At the end of the month we moved south again and the whole brigade was concentrated near the village of Alwinbyn on the Ngaukeydauk Chaung. Here we had our first dealings with the Royal Tank Corps and the 25th Dragoons came under command of 26 Division. We got to know the Dragoons very well and spent a great deal of time working out how best to combine with them in action and carrying out one or two small exercises. 4 and 36 Brigades were now south of us and 71 Brigade had a comparatively peaceful time apart from constant patrolling. A fairly large party of Tanabasha's forces was reported to be north-west of us. Two companies were sent out to form a stop while the Garhwals drove through the jungle. Unfortunately we were rather thin on the ground and a party of about fifty Japs who were led with great skill and dash managed to break through in the middle of a dark night. It is possible that they knew our positions for they chose the weakest part of the block and the first we knew of their arrival was a stream of red tracer followed by screams and yells as they charged through the two sections in their way. Some casualties were inflicted but the majority managed to get clear.

Everything was now fairly quiet on the Arakan Front. The main battle was being fought ta Kohima and Imphal right up in the north and it was not until towards the end of March that we again met the Japs in force. Early one morning a party of about four hundred were seen by the Garhwals making for the Wet Valley. This valley ran east and west for about two miles through the hills just south of Alwinbyn and had been made into a dry weather road. The enemy were quickly engaged by the Garhwals at the western end of the valley and the Lincolns were ordered to send two Companies to block the east end. The action in the Wet Valley was really a series of skirmishes lasting for about three days. The whole Battalion was finally engaged and it was our first real experience of working with tanks. The enemy had anti-tank mines and succeeded in catching two of our tanks and blowing off their tracks. By the end of the second day we had cleared the valley area up to the Garhwals to the west but the enemy still held a prominent hill overlooking the entrance to the valley. It was decided to make a deliberate attack on this hill supported by artillery and tanks. The Garhwals had made three gallant but unsuccessful attacks. The Commanding Officer detailed " B " Company, Major Varian, for this attack. The guns, including mediums, opened up well before Zero while the Company formed up and the tanks got into position. As the Company advanced through the thick jungle up the hill the tanks kept up a barrage of fire in front of them, firing as close as possible over their heads, changing to armour-piercing shell as they neared the top, to which the troops could get very close indeed. At a signal—we usually used Verey lights—from the Company Commander, which was given about fifteen yards from the crest, the tank fire lifted but continued overhead to discourage the Japs from lifting their heads, while the troops charged over the crest. Battalion Headquarters was on a small knoll just in rear, where there was a Tank Liaison Officer with a No. 17 wireless set in touch with the tanks so that their fire could be controlled as necessary. The attack went off like a drill and the hill was captured and Wet Valley was again clear of the enemy.

We continued to work like this with the 25th Dragoons and soon became so confident in each other that tanks could keep up a barrage of fire literally within a foot or so of the heads of the leading troops. We had very few casualties in this way and were no doubt saved very large numbers from the enemy. One man certainly bore no illwill for on a visit by the Tank Commander on one occasion to the field ambulance he was thanked by the wounded man with a cheery grin because it "saved him climbing to the top of the —— hill, anyway."

It was the Japanese habit to keep well down in their "bunkers" during the initial bombardment, where they were usually safe from anything less than a direct hit from a Medium. As soon as the guns stopped firing the enemy would emerge and meet our advancing troops with everything in his favour. With tank assistance our troops could now practically reach the enemy positions before the supporting fire was lifted and the enemy were forced to keep under cover.

The weather was now beginning to get unpleasantly hot and with the amount of motor transport now in the area, with tanks and carriers, the dust was appalling.

The enemy were still holding the area south of the Buthidaung road in considerable strength with a small pocket of resistance in a large area of jungle-clad hills just north of the road, known as the " Maze." A place known to be strongly held by the enemy was in the hills by the village of Dongyaung in the area where we had had our headquarters in 1943.

Battalion H.Q., 1st Battalion in action in Burma, 1944

It was decided that the Lincolns would capture these positions, staging the attack from their present harbour. Brigadier Cotterill-Hill called a conference of Commanders and started planning for the operation which was to be launched on a big scale with all possible support. The objective was to be two hill features known as " Spit and Polish." With the help of maps, air photographs and our knowledge of the ground from the previous year's operations, we made a complete sand model of " Spit and Polish." Several patrols were also sent out to reconnoitre the best tank routes. Mines were common and photographs showed one large tank obstacle and part of the ground was known to be boggy. Captain Lawson who had been Carrier Officer in 1943, and Captain Jack Munroe, the Tank Squadron Commander with whom we were working, took out the patrols in many cases right up to the enemy positions and brought back very valuable information. Captain Munroe later won the M.C. and was killed in Central Burma in 1945.

It was possible to get a good view of the objective and approaches from a hill near Buthidaung and all Company and Platoon Commanders were able to study this. The model was quite accurate and every single man who was to take part was briefed. The Commanding Officer detailed "A" Company, Major Innes, " C " Company, Major Wright, and " D " Company, Major Hill, for the attack. The artillery support consisted of practically all the guns in the Arakan, consisting of Mediums, 25-pounders, and 3.7 howitzers. The air were to dive-bomb the features before the artillery barrage and to do another mock attack to keep the enemy under cover while the infantry was going up the hills. Our squadron of tanks was in support. It was decided to move to an assembly area near the Buthidaung road during the night before the attack and to reach the forming-up line before dawn. The forming-up position was a chaung about a thousand yards north-east of the objective. This was quite near to other enemy positions and 36 Brigade had been asked to have a force in position in the chaung to the south to stop any enemy interference. The country between the forming-up line and the objective was flat and open and there was a danger that the advancing troops might be shot up from the flanks and rear. Features from which such fire might be directed against us were neutralised by special tanks, artillery and mortars. Battalion Headquarters was to remain in the chaung on the forming-up line with 2 48 sets and telephones for communications within the Battalion, a 22 set and telephone to Brigade and a tank Liaison Officer and a 17 set to the tanks. Lt. Colonel Williams-Wynn commanding 160 Jungle Field Regiment, R.A., was also with us in communication with the guns.

The Battalion, less Headquarters, Administration and " B " Company, moved by carrier to the assembly area on the late evening of April 6th and after a rest and a meal moved on by foot in the early morning of Good Friday to the forming-up line, the start of which was unmistakably marked by a very dead bullock, and arrived in good time. There was a long wait here under very good cover from view, as Zero had been fixed for 0800 hours to get the best results from air, artillery and tanks. Each Company had a 48 set and telephone and signallers were to reel out their lines, moving with the advancing troops. An Advanced Regimental Aid Post with Captain Battram and the Padre was also to move with the attacking Companies while a rear Regimental Aid Post with the medical Sergeant, Sgt. Page, was established further north. From here causalties were to be evacuated direct by motor ambulance to 46 Field Ambulance at Alwinbyn under Lt. Colonel Pace.

It was rather a trying wait on the forming-up line but before long we could hear the rumble of the tanks and they came into view, and at 2.20 we heard what sounded like a roll of thunder and a few seconds later " Spit and Polish" disappeared in clouds of dust and smoke. Previous to this we had watched a successful dive-bombing attack by Vengeance aircraft. The tanks soon got into their allotted positions and added their fire to that of the gunners. One tank was set on fire and destroyed by a Jap anti-tank gun which was itself soon put out of

(*L. to R.*) 2 Lt. Morris, Lieut. Miles, 2 Lt. Snelling.
The first two were killed a week later. April, 1944.

action. The smoke from the burning tank and the dust from the intense gunfire now completely blotted out the objective. The Commanding Officer got a message from the Squadron Commnader by wireless asking him to postpone Zero by five minutes to allow the dust to clear and make more accurate shooting possible, but he refused this and at Zero the three companies moved out of the chaung into the open and the advance started. The men having watched the apparently devastating fire started off in great form, slightly bunched at first but very quickly opening out and keeping a good, steady pace. Soon they came up to the tanks and passed through and began to disappear into the haze of dust and smoke, each company heading for its objective. " A " Company " Spit," " C " Company " Polish South" and " D " Company " Polish North." The tanks started to move up with the infantry keeping up a heavy fire with their 75 m.m. and Brownings. The Vengeance arrived in time to put in their dummy attack and the Companies started assaulting the hills through the jungle. They had crossed the open country safely and were storming the objectives when the enemy first saw them. It seemed impossible that there could be any enemy left alive, but they were still there in large numbers in their bunkers, dazed no doubt, but in most cases refusing to give in or withdraw as usual.   Reports began to trickle back, first by wireless and then telephone.   "A" Company had got " Spit" and had reached the top in time to bring a withering fire on the Japs withdrawing for once on the other side.   Casualties were fairly heavy.   Lieut. Morris, of "A" Company, had been killed and Major Innes wounded but remaining at duty.   " C " Company had found their hill more difficult, there being a second crest at which the tanks could not bring fire to bear.   They got half their objective.   They too suffered casualties.   Captain Miles and Captain Powell was killed and Major Wright wounded while leading an assault on the second crest.   " D " Company gained their objective but Major Hill was killed by a sniper and Lieut. Beale wounded.   Captain Lawson was in time and able to direct some very damaging gunfire on some enemy on the west of the hills, probably forming up for a counter attack.

The attack had gone in with great dash and courage.   The enemy had again been surprised, and suffered far greater casualties than ourselves, and the Battalion had again successfully carried out its allotted task.   Communications throughout were excellent and the Battalion Signallers under Captain Cheer were indefatigable, continually going out on foot or by carrier to repair lines and replace wireless sets.

Battalion Headquarters and the Defence Platoon now moved a few hundred yards north into an area held by one of the Battalions of 36 Brigade.   Tanks were withdrawn, wounded were being evacuated as quickly as possible, mostly by carriers, the crews and drivers of which did very fine work.

The Japs still continued to hold a part of " Polish" south and very little movement was possible on the objective.   The Companies consolidated as far as possible with what tools were available and were subjected to considerable enemy shelling and one or two counter attacks which were successfully repulsed.   Our air remained as active as possible to discourage enemy gunfire but they invariably opened up as soon as the skies were clear.

It had originally been decided that 36 Brigade would take over the positions that night but this had to be altered as we were ordered to remain on " Spit and Polish" until the night of the 8th.

The Companies spent a troubled and restless night and as soon as it was light the next morning enemy shell fire started again.   The Japs still held part of " Polish South" and Brigadier Cotterill-Hill agreed to send down a troop of tanks again to clear up the position. The Commanding Officer went down with them and met Major Innes who showed him the situation.   The tanks were manouevred into positions from where they could reach the enemy and proceeded to blow in the bunkers while " C " Company moved forward. In a short time the remaining Japs were destroyed.   The Commanding Officer now issued orders for the withdrawal that night and returned with the tanks to Advanced Battalion Headquarters.

The enemy kept up periodical shelling throughout the day and

The Chaplain (Rev. A. J. Pearson) preparing Communion Table after the action at Spit and Polish.

41

our own guns did what they could in counter battery work. The relief started at about 1900 hours but owing to confusion in the darkness took much longer than was expected, and Battalion Headquarters and " D " Company, the last Company to move, did not arrive back in Alwynbyn until dawn was breaking the following day.

General Lomax, whose headquarters was quite near, came with the Brigadier to see us in the morning and spoke to the whole Battalion and congratulated us on a very successful action which he said had probably been the biggest "killing" of Japs in any single operation in the Arakan. He spoke individually to many of those who had taken part and was lustily cheered on his departure. During the afternoon the Battalion moved to a new harbour a few miles to the west, bounded on the north by the Ngaukeydauk Chaung. Here on the evening of Easter Sunday the Padre held a thanksgiving and memorial service for those who had fallen.

CHAPTER VIII.

BUTHIDAUNG AND THE WITHDRAWAL.

The Supreme Commander, Admiral Lord Louis Mountbatten, paid a visit to the Arakan at this time and we were able to send a party of officers and men to meet him at the Divisional Administrative Headquarters in the old 7 Division Box. He was introduced to the party and then gave an informal talk on the situation in general in Burma.

Lord Louis Mountbatten also made a tour round the area and the Commanding Officer was detailed to describe to him on the actual ground the actions at Point 315 and at the west end of the Wet Valley. General Christison the Corps Commander was with the Admiral.

We stayed just over a week in our new harbour and during this time operations were carried out by the Punjabis and Garhwals and we were kept busy with a large area to patrol.

Our next move was to relieve 36 Brigade in the Buthidaung area and we took over our new positions on April 19th, back again in very familiar country. The Battalion was now well spread out. Headquarters and "C" Company, now commanded by Major Martin, were astride the Buthidaung road among some small hills known as "Defiles." "B" Company, Major Varian, held Buthidaung village, and "D" Company, Major Lawson, was north of the road and about a mile west of Headquarters on the south-west corner of Maze, the centre part of which was still held by the Japs. "A" Company, Captain Munroe, was about a mile further west in the hills above the iron bridge which had been so stoutly defended by "Tamil" in 1943. Brigade Headquarters with the Punjabis stretching south was about half-way between "A" Company and Battalion Headquarters and the Garhwals were holding an area south and slightly west of Buthidaung. This village was looking more dilapidated than ever, having been thoroughly bombed, shelled and occupied by both sides for well over a year.

It was now getting hotter and dustier than ever and the country that had been so much fought over was completely spoiled. Our time was taken up by constant patrolling in which we had many minor clashes with the enemy, frequently in "Maze" where he rather had the advantage in sitting inside and waiting for us.

Higher Command had decided that we should advance no further than the Buthidaung road and it soon became apparent that we were to withdraw again for the monsoon to a line further north, easier to hold and supply. The Buthidaung-Maungdaw road was still the only all-season motorable road south of Bawli Bazaar and the road north of this leading to Cox's Bazaar and Dohazari was very near second class and liable to be closed now and then during the monsoon.

Planning was soon started for the move back and everything not urgently required was gradually sent away. We were to move by night, leaving very small parties to hold various points to mislead the enemy. These were all composed of volunteers. A special deception unit also arrived who were to confuse the Japs for several days till the whole Division was well away to the north. The date fixed was the night of May 6th, exactly a year to the day since we withdrew from the same area in 1943.

On the night of the fourth we received information that the enemy were moving a gun from the east, possibly over the river just north of Buthidaung into "Maze." A fighting patrol under Lieut. Giardelli set out at about midnight to try and intercept this party, but unfortunately failed to make contact. The enemy gun was in fact not moved into "Maze" but into a position on a hill between "Defiles" and Buthidaung from where it could fire into our position. The only actual spot it could hit was the dugout used as the officers' mess and the officers' latrine. The Japs fired a number of shells and these places were not used again. Luckily only one officer, Captain Cheer, was sitting in the mess at the time and he spent some uncomfortable minutes lying on the floor.

As we were standing to on the morning of May 5th, the enemy who had broken through a small part of the Garhwals attacked Battalion Headquarters. Brigade Headquarters was also attacked at the same time, possibly both positions having been visited and "pin pointed" by members of the I.N.A. Some of the enemy were able to get right up to the perimeter, but were all killed and did not succeed in breaking through anywhere. For a short time the situation was rather confused as some Garhwals had withdrawn just in front of the Japs and it was not easy to tell friend from foe, and it is very possible that some of our own Indian troops were killed. We were now cut off from Brigade except by wireless and communications with "B" and "D" Companies were also only by wireless, though carriers could still dash through to both. Giardelli's patrol had tried to get in at much the same time as the enemy and in the confusion and fighting had a few casualties, Giardelli himself being wounded.

"A" Company had moved a few days previously and joined Headquarters and "C" Company. The Japs to the south had joined up to a certain extent with their force in "Maze." This was proved by the fact that in the kit of one of the attackers from the south was found a cigarette case belonging to one of the men who had been missing from a patrol that had had a fight in the "Maze" area a few days previously. The captured Jap equipment was mostly new and they were carrying a large supply of rations and it seems probable that they hoped to cut off the whole of 71 Brigade and had they been successful in over-running the two Head-quarters would possibly have succeeded.

There was still fortunately a force of tanks east of the Mayu Range and a troop was sent down to "Defiles" to help to drive the enemy back. On the 6th orders were received to draw in "B" Company from Buthidaung and to get the Garhwals concentrated into our area. With the help of the tanks, who on the way down to Buthidaung destroyed the Jap 3.7 which had been shooting us up in the rear, "B" Company were brought safely in with only a few casualties, some unfortunately from our own booby traps. The Garhwals moved next, again with tank support and met stiff opposition from the enemy amongst whom they and the tanks caused very heavy casualties. In time all the Garhwals arrived, with about eighty wounded, many of whom were brought in on our carriers. The Garhwal Medical Officer was missing and our Regimental Aid Post was hard pressed and overflowing. However, all the wounded, including our own, were finally evacuated by carriers along the Maungdaw Road to a com-paratively safe point when they were taken on by ambulance. The carrier crews and drivers again did exceptionally fine work and no one was more grateful to them that Colonel Farquarson commanding the 1/18th. The night was fairly quiet. The enemy had received a good battering and we were not in a position to take offensive action.

On the 7th we received orders by wireless from Brigade to withdraw to a point north of the Letwidet Chaung. The withdrawal was to start on the arrival of a squadron of tanks which was timed for 1700 hours. The Lincolns were to move first followed by the Garhwals. "D" Company was ordered by wireless to join on behind as we passed. All stores and ammunition had by this time been sent back and we only had with us what we could carry. The route was across open country for about two miles, but with tanks suitably placed it was hoped to keep down enemy small arms fire. Everything was ready in time and we moved off, spreading out when we reached the open, the Japs apparently making no serious effort to follow up. Just before we reached "D" Company's position the enemy opened up with what must have been every gun he had in the Arakan and we came under a greater concentration of gunfire than we had previously experienced. The tanks had succeeded in their main task and no small arms fire was directed at us. Shells from 75s and 105s were now falling thick amongst the Battalion and it looked as though we were going to have fairly heavy casualties. However, the Jap Artillery was more noisy than dangerous and we finally got out of the danger area to find later that we had only had one man killed. "D" Company, seeing the concentration of fire, had very wisely stayed where they were and slipped away and joined us later when things had quietened down. We soon reached our new position and before long got in touch by wireless with Brigade Headquarters to find that the remainder of the Brigade had got back safely with remarkably few casualties. The enemy made no attempt to follow us up and we spent a quiet night. The following day there was a certain amount of shelling, most of it falling rather to the west of us. We had orders to move back to Sinzweya that night, which we reached safely at about midnight to find a very welcome hot meal ready for us. We were now ordered to move further north to an area at Point 224 just East of Prinkaung and we marched again the following night. We were to stay in this position with a Battery of 3.7s until the monsoon broke, to patrol well south to give early warning of any Jap movements northwards and to fight a delaying action in the event of any determined advance. All motor transport was now moved back to the west of the Mayu Range and we reverted to an A.T. basis, being supplied from Goppe Bazaar. The new area was quite pleasant, comparatively fresh and easy to defend. Our patrol area extended southwards to the Ngaukeydauk Chaung and we invariably had two platoons well south who relieved each other on the ground. Smaller patrols worked east and west and north towards Goppe Bazaar. While we were here the West Africans of 81 Division began to pass through on the way back from their drive down the Kaladan Valley.

We were at Point 224 for about three weeks and wondering whether, and towards the end hoping, every storm would be considered by higher authority to be the proper monsoon.

The enemy made no move and on June 1st, sufficient rain having fallen we marched back to Goppe, bivouacked for the night and then continued over the pass to our monsoon quarters a few miles south of Bawli Bazaar. The monsoon had now started in earnest. On arrival, our new area was a most depressing sight, consisting of very poor and only partially finished bashas built into the sides of small hills, separated from each other by patches of paddy. Those of us who had been there had probably been spoilt by our previous year's rather attractive home at Nhila. Everyone was also rather weary and very wet.

CHAPTER IX.

THE MONSOON 1944.

We soon got down to making ourselves as comfortable as circumstances would permit and we had had some experience of this and knew what the monsoon meant in the Arakan. We had at times been referred to as The 10th Foot (web mark iii) as this was our third wet season in Bengal or Burma.

The first thing to do was to dig a system of drains at the same time building up and revetting bunds or footpaths about two or three feet high wherever it was necessary to cross over the low lying paddy ground. This was usually about six inches to a foot under water. Bashas had to be completed, strengthened and as far as possible made waterproof. Stands had to be prepared, with a very limited supply of stones, collected from the chaungs running out of the Mayu Range for motor transport and mules. At the same time defences had to be dug, revetted and roofed where necessary and our main defence position was about two or three miles north of the camp. Positions also had to be prepared round the camp itself. In addition to all this work we still had to cover the same patrol area as we had had at Point 224.

We had hoped to get considerable numbers away on leave but our minimum strength laid down by Corps Headquarters was too high to allow many to go. However, it was a relief to be able to dispense with the dawn and dusk stand-to and to be able to have limited lights at night in the form of hurricane lamps and to feel that we were separated from the Japs for a time by the Mayu Range though it was never safe to be too certain of this.

Patrols now became very arduous indeed. When possible they were lifted as far as Goppe Bazaar by motor transport but they were usually away for about four or five days and though they saw little of the enemy they lived in the greatest discomfort and were constantly wet through. The going was very difficult, the country was waterlogged and all the chaungs had swollen and were often impassable. In the hills jungle paths were sometimes washed away and there were several fatal accidents caused by men falling down steep khuds. In the jungle itself, everything was damp, steamy and soggy with the continual dismal drop of water from the leaves overhead. It was of course the season for leeches which no patrols could avoid, which often caused septic sores which took a long time to heal. Luckily, there were hot, dry and sunny spells now and then, when we managed to dry things up.

It was at Bawli Bazaar that we started our own canteen known as the " Poacher's Arms" with Major Homersham in charge. Captain Ryan had painted an inn sign which was erected at the entrance and swung and creaked in the wind in the correct way. We were able to buy stores, including tea, milk and sugar, in fairly large quantities from the C.B.I.D. which had a branch in Bawli Bazaar. We sold gallons of tea and the normal sort of supplies usually available in the N.A.A.F.I. and had to have a staff of four B.O.Rs. in charge as a whole time job. The " Poachers' Arms" was very popular and always full during opening hours and the wireless was kept going at full blast. We luckily had our own charging machine and could deal with the batteries. Though everything was sold practically at cost price it was impossible not to make a great deal of money which came in very useful for buying such amenities as wireless sets, gramophones and indoor games. Owing to the shortage of small change we had to have our own currency consisting of printed tokens.

Major Innes, who had just got a bar to his M.C. for his gallantry and leadership at " Spit and Polish," Major Martin and a little later Major Varian, all now well overdue for repatriation, left for England at about this time. This was the first batch of officers we had had to lose in this way, though there had been a constant drain with the other ranks during the whole of our time in the Arakan, naturally always composed of the oldest soldiers and usually N.C.O.s and specialists. Major Roissier now joined from Headquarters, 11th Army Group, later to become A.L.F.S.E.A., and was posted to the Battalion as Second in Command.

We were hoping at this time that we should be taken right out of the Arakan for a spell, but this was not to be and at the beginning of September we were ordered over the Mayu Range again to form the garrison at Taung Bazaar. This was a very strong, well dug and wired defensive position in the hills by the Kalapanzin River near the village. We had with us two batteries of gunners and a company of machine gunners. When the whole of 71 Brigade was again east of the Mayu Range, Brigade Headquarters joined us at Taung. Two Companies were detached, " D " Company at Point 224 and "A" Company near Badana East. Both these companies were in touch by wireless and telephone and acted as advanced bases from which to send out patrols. Here for the first time we used men of the Labour Corps as porters to carry out rations and supplies. The enemy became more active and patrolling was intensified, and we as usual kept the initiative and dominated the area.

We heard early in October that 4 Brigade was going to relieve us, but just before this happened, the Japs, moving through the jungle to the east of the Kalapanzin attacked Goppe Bazaar with a force of about two hundred. It seems certain that the enemy intelligence must have been at fault because they were completely outnumbered and suffered very heavy casualties. They were also probably new troops and certainly not up to the usual standard. In attempting to withdraw they passed fairly close to Taung Bazaar and were very successfully engaged by our guns who caught them in the open paddy and only a small proportion can have succeeded in getting back. They were of a certain nuisance value and managed to cut off our supplies which came by river from Goppe for a few days.

No attack was made on any of our positions, but just before we left the enemy moved some of his guns further north and shelled us for a bit but caused no casualties.

We were finally relieved on October 12th, and marched back to Goppe Bazaar where we were met by motor transport and taken to a basha built camp at Taungbro, not far from Tumbru Ghat. We were now in reserve and had a fairly restful time with much less patrolling.

Here we were visited by General Slim, G.O.C. in C. 14th Army, who gave us an hour's talk on the general situation in Burma. Afterwards he spoke to the Battalion alone. He was introduced to the Officers and Warrant Officers and spoke to many of the men. His visit and the speech he made to us were very much appreciated. We were still unable to get more than a very few away on leave, but General Lomax decided to move us further back to an area on the sea shore where we could have a real rest. At the end of the month, after a few reconnaissances, we moved to the new area. This was really a very pleasant place. We camped in the trees on the edge of the beach and we were told that we were not expected to do any work beyond arms inspections and anti-malarial parades in the evenings. The beach was of clean sand and broad and flat and stretched north and south for miles. We were able to make football, hockey and cricket pitches which were daily washed and rolled by the sea. Bathing was delightful, only sometimes slightly spoiled by the presence of stinging jelly fish and small rays. We had sports meetings and formed " The Arakan Turf Club" and had two race meetings with our mules as the runners. There was a rupee tote for each race which was crowded with Lincolns, Punjabis and Garhwals, all greatly enjoying a gamble. The " Poachers' Arms" re-opened and did a roaring trade. Everyone spent the days in shorts only and all skin diseases which had been getting rather serious gradually disappeared. The complete rest and recreation did the Battalion an enormous amount of good.

Other things were now being planned for us which were kept very secret and in the middle of November the Battalion moved under Major Roissier via Cox's Bazaar for an unknown destination and an unknown purpose. All Commanders stayed behind for planning, for which a large wired camp was erected. The Battalion had actually moved back into India to Coconada on the west coast north of Madras. The Combined Operations Training School was at Coconada and the Battalion was to do about six weeks' intensive training in this type of warfare. We found the new training very interesting and did several landings on the coast as exercises. General Sir Oliver Leese attended and on hearing from Brigadier Cotterill-Hill of our state as regards leave—many officers and men had not been away for over a year—agreed to a hundred and fifty going off immediately, which he said was partly due to the great spirit and dash with which the Battalion had carried out the exercises. This was very welcome indeed.

We spent Christmas at Coconada and everyone had a good time and supplies were plentiful. Unfortunately, as at Chittagong, we had another accident with a large basha and the whole area was well lit up on the night of Christmas Eve.

The Commanding Officer flew back again to the beaches to continue detailed planning and was lucky to get a lift and travel in great comfort with General Laycock in Lord Louis Mountbatten's private Dakota.

We were planning at this time for an assault on Akyab Island and the Battalion moved early in the new year back to Chittagong from which port we were to embark. We heard that the Japs had evacuated Akyab and that the island had been occupied by our troops without a fight and we now started planning again, this time for an assault on Ramree Island.

The Battalion continued training, concentrating mostly on marching with heavy kit. Feet needed toughening after the monsoon and rather wet training at Coconada.

Plans were completed in due course, but still secret to all, but a very few, and after many false alarms, postponements and cancellations, the Battalion at last embarked on S.S. *Land-stephan Castle* lying out to sea with the remainder of the transports off the mouth of the river. No one was allowed off ship, secrecy was no longer necessary and everyone was carefully briefed on maps, models and photographs. There was a great disappointment at first with the rations on board which were found to consist practically entirely of bully and biscuits. However, after a visit by General Lomax this was very quickly put right and for our remaining few days on board we did very well. We were paid a final visit by Sir Oliver Leese and sailed at night in a complete black-out and for the next few days were busy in rehearsing the drill for disembarkation into assault landing craft of which ten were carried on board.

CHAPTER X.

RAMREE.

The assault on Ramree was to be a daylight landing with strong Naval and Air Support. The Lincolns and 5/1st Punjab were the leading Battalions, Lincolns landing on the right on White Beach. The Garhwals were the follow-up Battalion and 4 Brigade were follow-up Brigade. "A" Company, Major Munroe, and "B" Company, Major Muse, were the two leading Companies to land at H hour followed by "D" Company, Major Homersham at H+5 and Battalion Headquarters at H+8. "C" Company, Major Davies with first reinforcements and a duplicate Battalion Headquarters were to land at H+30, followed as craft became available by the rest of the Battalion.

Battalion Headquarters though cut down to a minimum was large and grew after landing. Apart from the usual 22 sets and 46 sets for use in the Battalion and Brigade there were gunners and Tank Liaison Officers and on this occasion an F.O.B. for controlling Naval Guns and a V.C.P. to call for air support.

Two carriers were in the H+30 wave and a proportion of tanks were also to be landed at this time. The beach was good for landing but was reported to be wired and probably mined. Each Platoon carried a bangalore torpedo to destroy the wire. The Royal Navy, which included H.M.S. *Queen Elizabeth*, carried out a heavy preliminary bombardment while squadrons of Liberators attacked targets slightly inland and Thunderbolts and Spitfires strafed the actual beaches. We transferred to landing craft some miles out and were able to watch all this on the run in. The troops were in excellent form and there were many bursts of cheering as they passed the Headquarters L.C.P. to form up or when a particularly heavy load of bombs crashed down on the enemy. The run in was uneventful, though two of "A" Company's assault craft had temporary breakdowns and were late in touching down. We met with no under-water obstacles but two craft were blown up by these later in the day. There was very little opposition on landing and the first objective was gained according to plan without casualties. The opposition stiffened a bit as we got the second objective and "B" Company were held up for some time by enemy on Point 191. After an air strike on this hill we managed to get the third objective where we captured a 75 m.m. gun and by the evening of "D" day we were well established and supporting arms had been landed. "C" and "A" Companies sent out fighting patrols just before dusk to Black Hill and Mount Peter where they met fairly heavy opposition and suffered casualties. After this we settled down for the night and a supply of tins of self-heating cocoa arrived which we were able to distribute to all companies. Early next morning the advance continued, the Garhwals taking over Mount Peter on the right. "C" Company took Black Hill from which it was found that the enemy had withdrawn during the night. After a fairly slow start we pushed on south through the day until finally stopped by orders from Brigade Headquarters as we were outstripping our supporting arms. Some of the bridges had been blown on the only road and the sappers did marvellous work in getting them repaired or making diversions to enable tanks and guns to get well forward. The road also had to be cleared of mines in many places.

The country was very pleasant and as yet unspoilt by operations. The inhabitants we met seemed very pleased to see us and helped as far as they could in telling us where the enemy were. On D+1 we moved about fifteen miles which was quite good going as we were carrying heavy packs and two days, jungle pack rations. The Brigadier arrived just before dark and issued orders for the following day. The Garhwals moved through us just after dawn and we had an easy day advancing about four miles to Minbyn on the west coast where we stayed for the next twenty-four hours. Here we were able to examine the enemy defences which

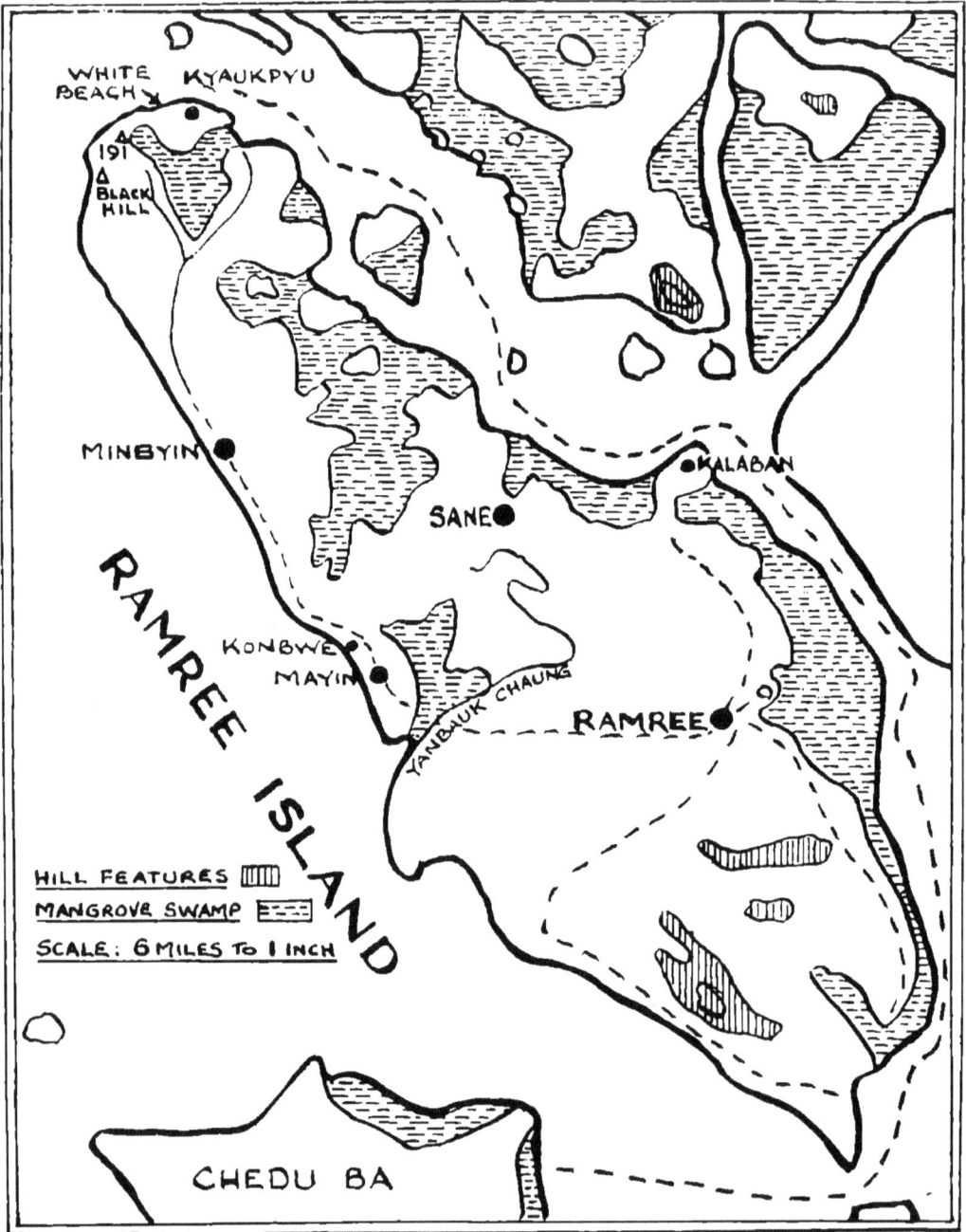

WHITE
BEACH
KYAUKPYU

191
BLACK
HILL

MINBYIN

MINBYIN

SANE

KALABAN

RAMREE ISLAND

KONBWE
MAYIN

YANBAUK CHAUNG

RAMREE

HILL FEATURES
MANGROVE SWAMP
SCALE: 6 MILES TO 1 INCH

CHEDU BA

were very well constructed and cleverly sited. The beach was mined, but the wire in many places was dummy, consisting of strands of creeper in place of wire which from air photos looked quite formidable.

We advanced again the next morning, passing through the Garhwals, with Konbwe as our objective, a village about twelve miles to the south. It was hot and hard work but we saw nothing of the enemy until the afternoon, when we struck him in a strong position on a ridge of hills not far from our objective. " C " Company were leading and moving across some open ground when the enemy opened fire with machine guns and mortars. They managed to push on well and gain a footing in the hills while " D " Company moved round to the left. We had a destroyer in support and the F.O.B. was able to bring fire to bear on the enemy but it was a difficult target and the shells were apt to go either well over or well short into the cliffs. " C " and " D " Companies managed to drive the Japs off the ridge and suffered a fair number of casualties. "A" and " B " Companies moved on to the objective under their cover and the Battalion took up a position on the hills overlooking the village just as darkness was falling. The two carriers managed to get through just before dark loaded with rations and cocoa, which were very acceptable after a long and tiring day. We had managed to keep the Japs on the move and everything was going well according to plan. General Lomax and the Brigadier arrived the next morning and it was decided to push the Punjabis through us and that we should move about three miles south to Mayin, another village on the west coast. Fighting patrols had gone out at dawn but failed to make contact with the enemy.

Casualties had not been heavy and it was good to have the Japs on the run. Rations were coming through well, we now began to get mail and " S.E.A.C." and morale was high.

We had a pause at Mayin and everyone managed to bathe after an area of beach had been cleared of mines.

The Japs, except for a few stragglers, had now all withdrawn south of Yinbaung Chaung where it looked as though they would make a final stand.

"A" Company were ordered to try and get across the Chaung a bit to the east in collapsible assault boats. They set out on this task and found almost insurmountable difficulties in getting themselves and their boats through a mile or so of mangrove swamp to the edge of the river. Major Munroe placed all his Bren guns on the river bank and attempted to get across in the boats only to be met with a withering enfilade fire from the enemy. One boat was sunk and of the two that got across one broke loose and floated downstream. The Jap fire was silenced by our own Brens and by gunfire from a supporting destroyer. The small party on the far side were with difficulty evacuated and the Company received orders to withdraw to Mayin.

Meanwhile the tanks had caught up and Brigadier Cotterill-Hill decided to push on to the east and north to cut off the enemy's line of retreat to the mainland. The Royal Navy were all this time keeping a sharp and frequently successful look-out for enemy craft trying to make a get-away to the east.

At the end of the month the Battalion had orders to move and to occupy the village of Sane which was well to the north-east. The Commanding Officer was also told that he must avoid heavy casualties. The Battalion started off before dawn and covered the greater part of the distance before mid-day when the Commanding Officer halted the Battalion and told " B " Company, who were leading, to send fighting patrols on ahead, as from information received from the Garhwals he expected to meet some enemy in the neighbourhood of Sane. Firing was presently heard in front, an enemy machine-gun post had been encountered and Lieut. Beattie in command of one of the patrols had managed to kill two Japs with his tommy gun. The patrols returned and enemy positions were pointed out and gunfire from the artillery and Royal Navy was brought down. One of the first 100-lb. shells from the Navy fell about 25 yards in front of the leading section, luckily doing no harm as the men were in a ditch. We now made a detour through the jungle, arriving at Sane just before dusk to find the Japs had left. We took up defensive positions, imposed a curfew on the villagers and signalled back that we had carried out instructions. The sappers and miners very quickly cleared a route for tracked venicles and the Brigadier arrived and told us we were now to push south and east, with the town of Ramree, the capital of the island, as our final objective. The Green Howards of 4 Brigade took over Sane. We moved south again and then east, passing

RAMREE ISLAND. Landing parties going ashore.

RAMREE ISLAND. Digging in on the first objective.

through the Garhwals, spending one night in "harbour" at another village called Minbyn. The Engineers were working hard in day and night shifts to clear a way for the tanks with great success. The following day we arrived again at the Yinbaung Chaung well to the east. This was overlooked by a hill feature, Point 233, and there was very little cover for approach. Patrols were sent out and found that the river was fordable near a village on the left and "A" Company were ordered to attack under cover of an air strike and artillery. The Company got through the village and about half-way up the hill when they encountered very heavy fire from the hill itself and from others within range and were held up. As it was not long before dark the Commanding Officer ordered the Company to withdraw back across the river and the Battalion occupied a defensive position in the hills near the north bank. Jap patrols were very active during the night and made several small bombing attacks on our positions, causing a few casualties and giving us a rather restless night. Major Duval, the Adjutant, and Captain West went back a short distance just after dark to meet a ration party and met a large Jap patrol but were fortunately in time to hide before the enemy passed within a few feet of them. They had only one pistol between them. The enemy had done a good bit of shelling during the day with a certain amount of success. The Commanding Officer got orders during the night to go back to Brigade Headquarters in the morning to discuss the situation. The Garhwals were to take the hills to the east, supported by tanks and when this was successful we were to take Point 233, which was to be heavily bombed. Oil bombs were to be used with high explosive which it was hoped would clear some of the thick jungle.

The Garhwals met heavy opposition and their advance was slow and the Commanding Officer was ordered to try and infiltrate across the river on to 233 during the air attack if he considered it possible. " C " Company were ordered to do this and taking every advantage of cover managed to reach the bottom of the hill while the bombing was in progress. The oil bombs were a great success and set fire to much of the undergrowth and the Japs must have decided temporarily to vacate their positions because " C " Company immediately followed by " D " occupied the hill before they could get back. Three of the missing, one badly wounded, from the previous day's attack were recovered. The whole Battalion now moved across the river and did some quick digging as the enemy were making use of their mortars. There were several counter attacks during the night and the enemy succeeded in gaining a footing on a ridge at the south-east corner of the feature and it was not until the afternoon of the following day that we were able to clear him off again. It was a very disturbed night with the jungle still burning and the enemy very active. The Garhwals were slowly pushing on on our left and before long we were able to advance again and struck the new Jap dry weather road leading to Ramree. The Punjabis pushed on up this for a few miles when we were ordered to move through them and to take Ramree. The tanks were up with us now and we moved on with one troop until about mid-day when we came to cross tracks and a place where the road had a right-angled bend. This was dominated by a thickly covered hill where the enemy had sited several machine guns posts with his usual skill and the exact position of which it was quite impossible to spot. "A" Company, now commanded by Major Cheer, as Major Munroe had been wounded, attempted to push on to the right, but were held up and " D " Company were sent round to the left. The tanks could not get past the bend as it was impossible to clear the road of mines until the enemy had been driven back. " D " Company did well and managed to clear several of the bunkers and indicate others which were taken on by fire from the tanks. The Navy and artillery also gave supporting fire but the Japs were making their last stand and were obviously going to die in the positions they held. "A" Company again lost their Company Commander when Major Cheer was wounded and Captain Nevile took over. Captain Battram, the Medical Officer, was also hit when trying to extricate some wounded. Darkness was approaching and the Commanding Officer concentrated the Battalion in defensive positions for the night which was comparatively quiet.

At dawn " D " Company pushed on again and " C " Company moved round to the right and managed to capture a hill in rear of the enemy who continued to hold on and block the only road to Ramree. The fight went on throughout the day, each bunker having to be destroyed in turn and the Battalion again concentrated for the night, leaving " C " Company on the hill behind the enemy. At dawn " C " Company made a drive back towards the Battalion through the enemy positions and " B " Company moved through " D " Company

53

round to the left and the advance was continued along the road to Ramree. Enemy snipers remained in the area for many days afterwards and a Company had to be kept there for some time. We reached Ramree about mid-day to find the town clear of Japs and we took up our new positions.

Ramree was a pleasant little town full of temples and pagodas and though neglected was not very badly damaged by our air. We entered the town on February 9th, exactly twenty days after landing at Kyaukpyu. The tanks were with us which was a very good effort on the part of all concerned considering the obstacles that had to be overcome. All organised resistance was now at an end and we spent the next few weeks rounding up enemy stragglers who continued to hide in the jungle.

The local population began to come back and an official ceremony was held on Pagoda Hill where the Commanding Officer had the honour of hoisting the Union Jack over Ramree.

C.A.C.S.

The Battalion remained in Ramree "town" for about two weeks. This period was mainly a rest, with occasional ambush patrols being sent out into the jungle to waylay small parties of Japanese who were trying to make their way to the coast and so over to the mainland.

After this short rest the Battalion was moved to the Kalabon area in the North East corner of the island. The task was to round up any parties of Japanese escaping through the mangrove swamps. Kalabon area was mainly mangrove swamps with one ridge of high ground, rising to some 300 feet, running inland and down the East coast. The Battalion, less three companies, was based near the one beach suitable for landing craft, the remaining companies were disposed over an area up to eight miles distance. It was extremely hot and humid, water was scarce and mainly supplied from shallow holes dug in the swampy soil. Rations were brought daily by L.C.M. from Ramree town ; this entailed a two-three hour trip up various chaungs to the Battalion base ; thence they were sent out to companies by porters recruited from the local inhabitants.

Patrolling was continuous, including searches of neighbouring small islands. Many indications of recent Japanese occupation were found, but during the three weeks that the Battalion was in that area a few Japanese were captured ; these were poor specimens and in very bad health, having been living in the swamps for about two weeks without food in most cases.

At the end of three weeks the Battalion returned to Ramree town for a few days, then moved back to Gonchwein, near Kyaukpyu, preparatory to sailing to India for leave and refitting.

On 24th March, Lt. Col. C. A. C. Sinker, D.S.O., left the Battalion for leave in England and Major D. P. St. C. Roissier, then second in command, took over command of the Battalion.

On the 27th March the Battalion embarked and sailed for Madras in H.M.T. *Dunera*. All ranks were in great spirits at the prospect of the long promised leave in India. The voyage was uneventful and the convoy arrived in Madras harbour on 1st April. The whole Brigade group, less the 1/18 Royal Garhwal Rifles who were temporarily under command of 4th Indian Infantry Brigade for the Taungup operations, were in this convoy.

Suspicion should have been aroused when, with leave so near, the convoy arrived in India on "April Fool's Day." No sooner had the service units started to disembark than orders were given for the disembarkation to stop ; those who had disembarked were ordered to re-embark at once. Meantime the Lincolns, who were to have disembarked the following day, were on a route march through Madras, so they did at least set foot in India. Orders were given for the convoy to return to Ramree Island, but no reason for this move was given, which naturally caused great disappointment to all ranks.

In the evening of 4th April the convoy anchored off Kyaukpyu. The Battalion disembarked the following morning and marched to the same camp that it had left only nine days before.

Japanese 3.7m.m. A Tk. gun captured at Ramree by the 1st Battalion. (*L to R*).   SGT. R. HOLGATE, C.S.M. B. CARTER, PTE. H. TAYLOR.

C.S.M. STURGESS inspects the captured A Tk. gun.

General Sir Oliver Leese, C.-in-C. A.L.F.S.E.A., spoke to the senior officers about the forthcoming operation which necessitated the recalling of 71 Indian Infantry Brigade. The men were told an important operation was to take place ; for security reasons they could be given no details.

The whole of 26 Indian Division moved to a concentration area in the Myinbyin beaches, about fifteen miles south of Kyaukpyu, where planning and general preparations for the operation were started.

The maximum amount of E.N.S.A. and cinema shows were brought up for the troops, together with extra rations and other amenities ; these, together with the arrival of re-fitting stores and the bustle of preparations, soon caused the men's spirits and morale to return to their normal high state.

Admiral Lord Louis Mountbatten and General Sir Oliver Leese spoke to all units individually. It was pointed out that the operation was to be a race against time, apart from the Japanese, for the South West Monsoon was due soon when seaborne operations in small craft may be made impossible.

On 27th April, 26 Indian Division started to embark at Kyaukpyu. The main body of 1 Lincolns embarked in H.M.S. *Persimmon*, a L.S.I., whilst the follow-up troops of the Battalion embarked in H.M.T. *Dunera*. It was made known there to all ranks that the objective was Rangoon.

CHAPTER XI.

RANGOON AND RETURN TO INDIA.

Briefly, Rangoon had been chosen as the immediate objective for the following reasons :—

14th Army, under General Slim, was advancing from Mandalay, and was outstripping its supply lines owing to the difficult country and lack of roads for heavy vehicles ; also, there were insufficient aircraft available to maintain so large a force by air during the monsoon season. If the Japanese made a determined stand north of Rangoon the situation on that front would be grave. Rangoon was the only port in the south of Burma and, if captured, could be used as a base for a force to contact 14th Army and so supply them by sea. It was also known that the Japanese were withdrawing fast towards Malaya ; thus, if Rangoon was taken there might be a chance of cutting the Japanese line of withdrawal.

The only troops available immediately for this operation were those of 26 Indian Division. This operation developed into a race between this Division and the 14th Army as both were determined to be the first into Rangoon ; 14th Army because it would complete their capture of the Irrawaddy Valley and delta ; for 26 Indian Division it would complete the capture of the coast of Burma by troops of 15 Indian Corps.

The convoy sailed from Ramree Island on 30th April in pre-monsoon weather of showers, heavy squalls and a fairly choppy sea. The "slow convoy" that had sailed three days earlier was overtaken on 2nd May ; the whole then moved on and anchored some 25 miles off the mouth of the Rangoon river. Anchoring this distance out was necessary on account of the shallow water and unswept mine fields at the mouth of the river.

The plan for the assault entailed the heavy gun positions at Elephant Point, covering the river mouth, being captured by a battalion of paratroops of the Gurkhas on the evening of D-1. On D-day all available aircraft were to bomb and ground strafe the Japanese strong points and gun positions on both banks of the Rangoon river. The assault was to be made by 36 Indian Infantry Brigade on the West bank simultaneously with the assault of the East bank by 71 Indian Infantry Brigade. The 4th Indian Infantry Brigade was to be in reserve.

1/Lincolns were given the task of forming the initial beachhead on the East bank ; one company of 5/1 Punjab Regiment was placed under command of 1/Lincolns for the initial assault.

On D-day, 2nd May, 1946, the weather conditions were most uninviting with heavy rain and a big swell with squalls at sea. The run-in to the beaches was to be 25-30 miles which must be one of the longest on record for any operation of the war.

The assault troops of the Battalion embarked in the L.C.A. at 0130 hours and took the water at 0140 in a heavy rainstorm that continued most of the night. At dawn one saw many green faces in the various craft, but by then the craft were running into the more smooth waters of the Rangoon river where physical feelings returned to normal.

About 45 minutes before H-hour (0730 hours) the weather cleared and the air attack went in successfully. Elephant Point had been captured and no opposition was seen on the river banks.

1/Lincolns landed at the mouth of the Hwawnun Chaung, 15 miles south-east of Rangoon. The "beach" was a bank of deep mud with flooded paddy fields beyond. " C " and " D " Companies landed on the North bank, closely followed by Tactical Headquarters ; meantime "A" Company landed on the South bank to protect the rear of the beach-head.

Troops coming ashore for the capture of RANGOON, May, 1945.

As a village near RANGOON burns, stretcher bearers bring back wounded across the open plain.

No opposition was encountered during the assault and the initial objectives were quickly overrun. " B " Company was passed through the beach-head and secured Nandawnguswet, where three coastal defence guns were captured. The Battalion then moved forward to the area of Thilawa, four miles up the river bank ; meantime the remainder of the brigade had landed.

Transport had been unable to land at the original beach owing to the deep mud and flooded paddy fields, so all the "landing reserves" of ammunition, rations and 3-inch mortars had to be manhandled forward through deeply flooded paddy fields for the first 48 hours.

The advance was uneventful and the brigade concentrated at Syriam on D+2, from where Rangoon city could be seen the other side of the main river. On D+3 71 brigade crossed over to Rangoon city, and by the evening of 5th May the bulk of 36 and 71 Indian Infantry Brigades had moved into Rangoon.

71 Indian Infantry Brigade was ordered to move north of the city. Lincolns moved off first and took up temporary positions in Jacob Barracks at Mingaladon, 14 miles north of the city ; these barracks were the old pre-war British barracks, and were still in good condition. Patrols were sent out to locate Japanese forces reported in the area, whilst preparations were made to contact 14th Army. A few small parties of Japanese were located but on being engaged withdrew hastily outside patrol and gun range ; this was further evidence of the failing morale of the Japanese. Whilst at Mingaladon units of the 2nd Division of the Indian National Army were paraded and disarmed by the Lincolns ; the personnel were then sent to Insein gaol in Rangoon. Many of the I.N.A. had taken an active part in the fighting in North Borneo against British and Indian troops.

Many Allied prisoners of war were found in Rangoon together with a number of civilian internees. They were all in a very bad state of health and were immediately flown or shipped out to India. Rangoon was in a filthy state, all the better houses and buildings had been looted by the Burmese and Chinese, most of the Churches had been desecrated by the Japanese, public services and the main water supply system were out of order ; this together with the filthy and diseased state of most of the natives made one glad to be out of the city.

The Japanese flag that was flying over Government House when the Allies entered Rangoon was given to the Lincolns. This flag has been presented to the Regimental Museum at the Depot, Lincoln.

Information was received that elements of 14th Army were at Lhegu, fifteen miles North-East of the Lincolns. On 8th May, "A" Company, an Engineer mine clearing party, the Brigadier (H. P. L. Hutchinson) and the Commanding Officer went forward and contacted the 3/7 Gurkha Rifles of the 4th Indian Corps, who had been advancing from Tongoo. On the way to make contact some sniping and roads prepared for demolition were encountered, but otherwise there was no incident.

Having made contact with 4th Indian Corps it was decided then to move up the Rangoon-Prome road to the West and contact 33 Indian Corps, which was advancing down the Irrawaddy valley. It was known there was a considerable force of Japanese in the triangle formed by the two 14th Army Corps and 26 Indian Division ; but in spite of constant deep patrolling little contact with the Japanese was made, they preferring to withdraw rather than fight. One brief encounter did occur, however, when the Battalion Defence Platoon, under command of Lt. Wighton, contacted about 75 Japanese marines who had landed from a motor launch in the early morning near Myauntanga. The Japanese had the advantage of the thick cover along the river bank, whereas the Defence Platoon had to move over open paddy fields. A sharp action took place in which the Defence Platoon suffered three men killed and three wounded. The enemy casualties were heavy but they managed to regain their motor launch just before a patrol of 5/1 Punjabs and a troop of tanks arrived on the scene.

At the same time as this encounter took place, a fighting patrol from " C " Company with one troop of tanks, 19th Lancers, moved north to contact 33 Corps. Contact was made at milestone 61 with the 9/14 Punjab and armoured cars of the Carbineers.

On 16th May, the Lincolns and Brigade Headquarters were concentrated at Taikky, fifty miles north of Rangoon. Here further elements of the Indian National Army were disarmed, and active patrolling carried out to locate Japanese who were making their way into the thick jungle country to the east.

1st Battalion the Royal Warwickshire Regiment, from 4th Indian Infantry Brigade, arrived in the area preparatory to taking over from the Lincolns, who were due to leave on the first convoy back to India, having completed their task.

It may be of interest that due to the lack of transport (the Brigade transport was still held up in Syriam, and did not rejoin the unit until Taikky) Rear Battalion Headquarters was usually 25-35 miles behind the main body of the Battalion, the only transport in the Battalion at that time for transporting rations, ammunition and personnel were one broken down and aged civilian bus together with an equally decrepit ten-horse-power car.

On 18th May the Battalion moved back to Rangoon by road and "rail." The Royal Engineers, by a process of cannibalisation, had managed to get one old engine and twelve open flats moving on the railway between Rangoon and Hmawbi, a distance of twenty miles. This train did the return trip once per day. On this contraption half the Battalion entrained at noon ; after stopping four times to fill the engine with water, using a chain of ration tins to nearby pools or streams, and for the man to chop wood for the engine furnace, the train arrived at its destination at 6 o'clock in the evening.

On arrival in Rangoon the Battalion was put into a transit area until 21st May, and placed under command of 4 Indian Infantry Brigade for the move to India. All ranks spent most of the time sightseeing, in particular the many famous pagodas in the city.

H.M.T. *Dunera*, that had been associated closely with the Battalion since the Ramree landing, asked " Movements" that their ship might have the honour of carrying the Lincolns to India. It was a fine gesture much appreciated by all ranks. The request was granted and the Battalion embarked on 21st May. At the end of the voyage a Japanese battle flag was presented to the ship by 1/Lincolns.

The voyage back to India was uneventful and in perfect weather. Madras was reached in the evening of 24th May ; this time the Battalion did disembark, entrained that evening and arrived in Bangalore the following evening.

CHAPTER XII.

THE MOVE TO SUMATRA AND OCCUPATIONAL DUTIES AT PADANG AND PALEMBANG.

The Lincolns were stationed in " Y " Tank Camp, ten miles outside Bangalore. Soon after settling in the whole Battalion was sent on leave to various hill stations in South India.

Leave over, a bitter blow hit the unit. The Repatriation and Release Schemes were put into effect with the result that over fifty per cent of the Battalion left ; this included all the senior officers, all C.S.Ms, over fifty per cent of the N.C.Os, and some 250 men. The majority of those remaining were recent reinforcements with little training ; this combined with the low numerical strength of the unit resulted in the Lincolns being withdrawn from 26th Indian Division and posted to 109 L. of C. Area in Bangalore, in G.H.Q. (India) Reserve.

Operations for the final assault on Malaya were in preparation, but these plans had to be changed completely with the surrender of Japan on 15th August. South East Asia Command had to include now the Netherland East Indies, Hong-Kong, Siam and parts of Borneo in its new occupational areas.

26th Indian Division was allotted Sumatra as its occupational area. All ranks of the Lincolns felt that the Battalion was entitled to take part in the final round up of the Japanese. Requests were made that the Battalion might take a part in the occupational duties, and on 10th September 1/Lincolns were reposted back to 71 Indian Infantry Brigade. Time was short and the Battalion had only one week in which to completely refit, whereas the rest of the Division had been refitting for nearly two months.

On 26th September the brigade moved by rail to Trivalor, thirty miles from Madras, preparatory to embarking at that port. "A" Company embarked that day in L.S.T. 346 that was calling at Colombo before rejoining the convoy, but it was not until 4th October that the remainder of the Battalion embarked in H.M.S. *Prince Albert*.

The voyage to Sumatra was uneventful, and, owing to no war-time restrictions regarding blackout, was more comfortable than hitherto. For the first time since the South African War a Battalion of the Lincolnshire Regiment crossed the equator. Thanks to the Royal Navy the usual peacetime ceremonies at " Neptune's Court" were carried out to mark the occasion.

Information regarding the Japanese, the Indonesians and the political situation in Sumatra was very brief. It was reported that there were some 70,000 Japanese troops on the island, concentrated mainly in the Medan, Pedang and Palembang areas ; it was supposed that they were peaceful minded and would not offer any opposition. Nothing was known, then, of the Indonesian attitude towards the allied forces. Normal precautions were taken, therefore, in case there was any opposition from either source.

Detachments of Force 136 (mainly an intelligence force) and Red Cross had been parachuted and flown in prior to the landings of the main forces. These detachments were to give aid to the prisoners of war and internees in the interior of the island and fly out as many as possible. They reported that all their areas were quiet, and that the majority of the allied prisoners of war had been evacuated by air.

Headquarters of 26 Indian Division and 71 Indian Infantry Brigade were to occupy Padang, whilst 4 Indian Infantry Brigade was to occupy Medan. 1st Battalion The Burma Regiment was attached to the Division and moved in to guard the internees at Palembang.

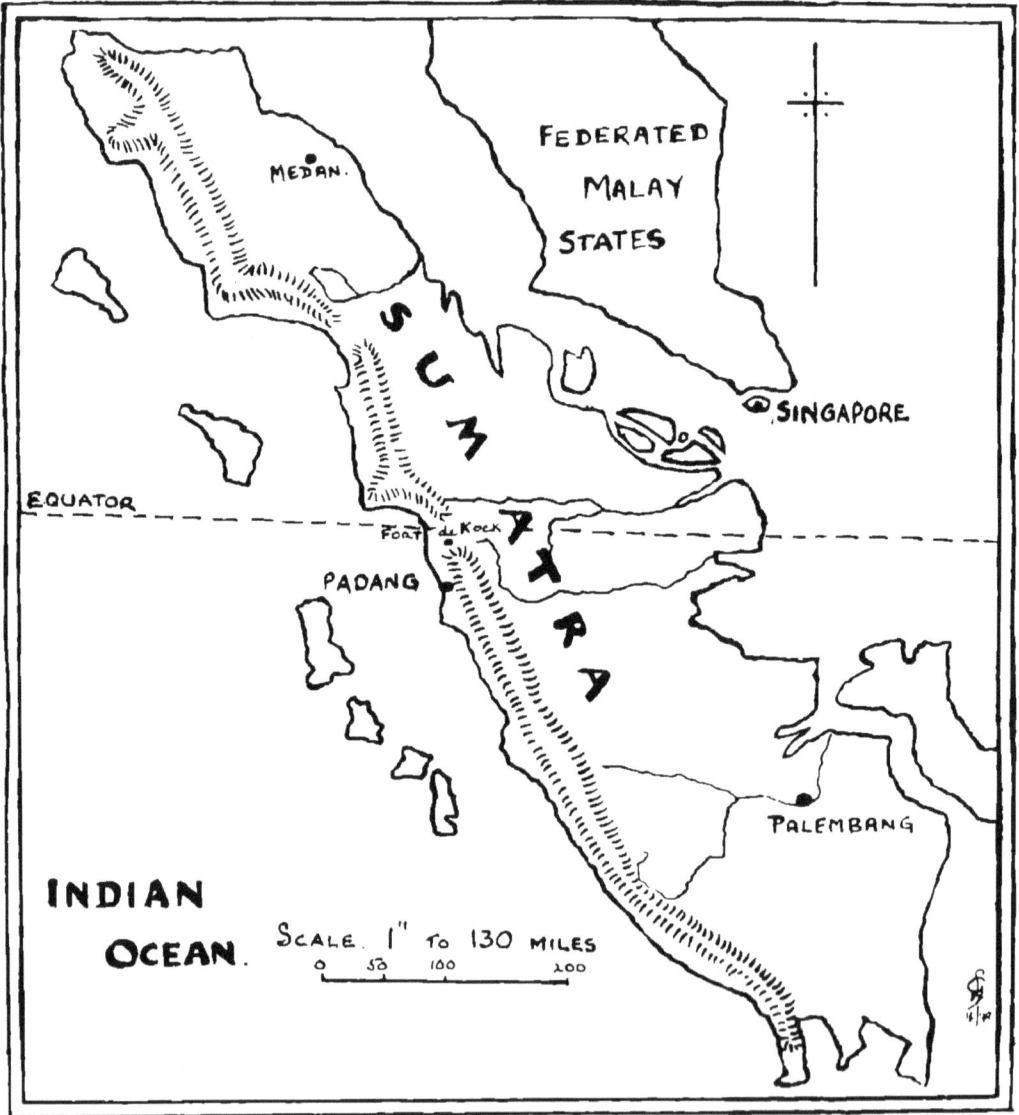

MEDAN.

FEDERATED
MALAY
STATES

SINGAPORE

S U M A T R A

EQUATOR

FORT de KOCK

PADANG

PALEMBANG

INDIAN
OCEAN.

SCALE. 1" TO 130 MILES

0   50   100   200

Padang owed its importance, apart from the internees, to being the main trade centre for Central Sumatra, also it controlled the largest cement works in the N.E.I. and one of the two coal mines in the island. Fort de Kock, seventy miles inland, was the seat of religious and political feelings of the Indonesians in Sumatra, and had been the Dutch capital until that was moved to Medan. The town lay on the coast in the centre of a coastal plain some forty miles by twelve miles, surrounded on the landward side by jungle covered mountains rising to 6,000 feet. There was the small port of Emmahaven, six miles to the South and a small airfield eight miles to the North. Being only thirty miles South of the equator, it was very hot, humid and subject to heavy tropical rain most of the year. There were some 300 European houses, the remainder of the town being mostly native design. The town was surrounded by native villages (Kampongs) inhabited by time-honoured thieves and trouble makers.

After a conference between the Senior British Naval Officer and the local Japanese Naval commander the convoy anchored near Emmahaven on 10th October.

The 1/18 Royal Garhwal Rifles landed first and covered the port. 1/Lincolns then landed and in trucks and a train, driven by Japanese, moved on to the town of Padang.

The reception by the Indonesians was cordial though cold, but no trouble was encountered in the initial occupation of the areas allotted in the town, which were all occupied by that evening.

There were about 4000 Dutch and Dutch Nationals who had been interned by the Japanese ; this figure was increased as more were brought in by the Red Cross from camps further inland ; about thirty per cent of these internees were children. All were in a poor state of health and clothing ; this state soon improved with the supplies of medical stores, food, and clothing brought in by the Civil Affairs officials. These internees were scattered all over the town, so for security, they were organised into two main areas each decently housed, holding about 3000 persons. These areas were guarded by Lincolns whilst the outlying vital points were the task of the Garhwals.

Owing to the size of Sumatra and the small Allied force that had been landed, certain vital areas inland were still left to the Japanese to safeguard until such time as they could be taken over by the Allies. These areas were mostly oilfields, food and Japanese army store dumps. Thus the extraordinary situation arose where recent enemies became semi-allies pending their return to Japan. An area of twelve miles radius round Padang was declared Allied occupied territory and all Japanese less a small liaison mission were cleared from this sector of the island ; martial law was proclaimed within this area.

The official surrender ceremony of the Japanese in Sumatra was held in Padang on 21st October, 1945 ; for this the 1/Lincolns provided a guard of honour.

Soon it became evident that there was very bad feeling amongst the Indonesians regarding the Dutch. The Indonesians, fostered by the Japanese during the past three years and to varying degrees armed by the Japanese, demanded " Freedom " and independence from Dutch rule. The arming of the Indonesian "army" (the T.R.I.) had not been so extensive in Sumatra as in Java. Later it became obvious that a fair number of Japanese had deserted their forces and were leading and training the Indonesians.

Though the few better educated Indonesian leaders realised that although they might get their independence, the Indonesians would have to rely on Dutch or Allied technical help and advice, the uneducated masses demanded complete freedom and independence. This latter feeling grew to include resentment of any interference by the Allied forces.

Early in November the first active Indonesiasn demonstrations occurred. These took the form of attempts to murder Dutch individuals who had gone outside the protected internee areas, against orders. Widespread propaganda in the form of blood curdling posters appeared all over the town. Attempts were also made to break into the internee areas and kidnap children with the intent to murder them later. All attempts to kidnap internees were prevented by the British troops, though there were several instances of kidnapping large parties of Chinese who lived outside the protected areas ; these were accused of being pro-Dutch in their views and activities. Isolated instances continued day and night. Frequent raids, varying from a few soldiers to two or three companies of British troops, were carried out both by day and night.

These threw a big strain on the unit which had to guard the Dutch personnel as well with a unit strength of about 500 men ; however, the variety of tasks was welcomed by all ranks, and these raids resulted in a large number of bad characters and ringleaders, besides small dumps of arms and explosives being captured. The Indonesians used mainly knives for stabbing, but small arms and grenades were frequent in later stages, in particular at night. They suffered many casualties, but the Battalion's casualties in Padang only amounted to one B.O.R. killed and one wounded.

On 4th December the Brigade-major and a Red Cross girl were foully murdered by the Indonesians near Emmahaven ; prior to this two British merchant seamen had been murdered in the same area. After three days of intensive raiding and searching by the Lincolns and the Field Security detachment the bodies were found. It was proved that several villages had been implicated in these crimes. Therefore, these villages, extending over some six miles of the coast, were burned to the ground as a reprisal. Apart from a few small incidents there were no more major crimes or disturbances in Padang during the time the Battalion was there.

Christmas, 1945, was well celebrated and enjoyed by all ranks, it being the first Christmas for many years that the Battalion had been decently housed and had full facilities for parties and dances.

Early in the new year, 1946, large numbers of Dutch internees were evacuated to Holland ; those remaining were concentrated into one area, likewise the Lincolns were concentrated to guard them, thus easing the duties considerably.

On 12th March orders were received that the Battalion was to fly to Palembang the following day. No warning of an air move had been given and it was the first time the Battalion had moved by air. However, after a hasty packing up of the unit stores the first fifteen Dakota loads flew out on 13th March. The whole Battalion, less a baggage party who were to move by sea, was moved in three lifts and was concentrated in Palembang by the 15th March.

On arrival at Palembang one company took over the protection of the airfield, ten miles outside the town. The remainder of the Battalion was concentrated in the Fort in the town. The duties of protecting the Dutch internees was still carried out by 1 Burma Regiment.

It had been decided that Palembang, with the oil producing country surrounding and the two large oil refineries (" Shell " and " Standard ") at Pladjoe and Soengi Garong, six miles down river, was a more important place economically than Padang. Soon after arriving, Headquarters 71 Indian Infantry Brigade moved to Palembang to command that area. Lt. Col. Roissier was ordered back to Padang to command that area until such time as a new sub-area headquarters could be brought in ; Major W. J. R. Cragg took over temporary command of 1/Lincolns.

Palembang was peaceful when the Battalion arrived, but it was obvious that trouble was not far distant. Until this time all areas in Palembang, except the Dutch ex-internees, had been guarded and patrolled by the Japanese. There had been no Allied control of Indonesian activities or any definite Allied Occupied area laid down. As soon as the British troops took control of the area the "Anti-Allies" propaganda became widespread.

At the end of March two small escort parties of 1/Lincolns were ambushed in the native area of the town when returning from the naval jetty ; there were no casualties to the troops. The following day, 30th March, a Lincoln road patrol under command of 2/Lt. Bayliss was seriously ambushed on the edge of the town. The patrol was surrounded by heavy fire from buildings including a mosque that had been fortified by the Indonesians. The patrol was caught in the open streets with no cover, but managed to fight its way back to some three-quarters of a mile from the fort. A relief company was sent out from the fort and a sharp battle ensued in the middle of the town, about 800 yards from the fort. Eventually the patrol was relieved and all troops withdrew to the fort and heavy mortar fire was concentrated on the Indonesians who dispersed. Lincolns suffered three other ranks killed, two officers and nine other ranks wounded. The Indonesians admitted to over 100 casualties, mostly killed. Meantime a British ship moving to the coaling station two miles up river was engaged by an Indonesian "Army" training camp on the banks of the river ; this camp was severely dealt with by a Royal Navy landing craft gun and two motor launches.

Lord Louis Mountbatten inspects the Guard of Honour of the 1st Battalion
at PALEMBANG, Sumatra, 25th April, 1946.

That was the last of the Indonesian major incidents in Palembang. One week later the Indonesian " Resident" asked the Lincolns to play the Indonesians at football to promote more friendly feeling. This game was watched by about 3-4000 Indonesians, who also produced a band ; the Lincolns won 4—0 after a very clean game.

For the remainder of the time in Palembang the Battalion duties consisted mainly of anti-looting guards.

Prior to relinquishing command of S.E.A.C., Admiral Lord Louis Mountbatten visited Palembang, 26th April. He congratulated the Lincolns on their extremely smart guard of honour, also on the way the Battalion had carried out all its tasks in Burma and Sumatra.

In mid-June, Lt. Col. Roissier returned to the Battalion from Padang.

Early in July the evacuation of the Japanese from this area started. The 3/4th and 3/9th Gurkhas arrived from Malaya to take over the town and airfield protection. At the same time 1/Lincolns and 1/Burma Regiment were moved down river to take over the protection of the oil refineries. The Lincolns were given the task of preventing sabotage and protecting the Dutch technicians in the " Shell " refinery at Pladjoe. Apart from interference of small parties of thieves who worked mainly by night, there were no incidents with the Indonesians.

Guard duties were extremely heavy as the refinery had a perimeter of about four-and-a-half miles apart from the many installations to be guarded. Pladjoe was, however, a pleasant place compared with the fort ; there were good houses and facilities for games, cinema and swimming pools.

In August it was announced that the Dutch troops would take over the areas occupied by the British, the hand-over to be completed by the end of November, also that after the relief, 26 Indian Division was to be disbanded and 1 Lincolns were to move to Malaya.

Early in October advanced parties of the Dutch forces arrived and preparations were made for the hand-over. There was no interference from the Indonesians, due mainly to the able diplomatic handling of both the Dutch and Indonesians by the British formation commanders.

65

On 20th October, Lt. Col. R. H. L. Oulton arrived from England to take over permanent command of 1 Lincolns from Lt. Col. Roissier who left for England on repatriation at the end of October.

The complete hand-over of the Palembang and refinery areas went smoothly without a shot being fired by either side.

The 1st Battalion the Lincolnshire Regiment left Palembang about 8th November and moved to Taiping, Malaya, where they were to come under command of 49 Indian Infantry Brigade in 23 Indian Division.

So ended the operations by the 1st Battalion the Lincolnshire Regiment against the Japanese in Burma, and the subsequent operational duties in the areas that had been occupied by the Japanese.

With the exception of the four months spent in Bangalore in 1945 this battalion had been in the operational areas, the majority of the time in active operations, for nearly four years.

D. P. St.C. R.

OFFICERS, 1st BATTALION ROYAL LINCOLNSHIRE REGIMENT. TAI-PING, MALAYA. JANUARY, 1947.

Lt. J. Mills. Lt. E. C. Whitby 2 Lt. N. L. Williams Lt. J. W. Renders 2 Lt. T. A. Twigg 2 Lt. H. R. Jarvis
2 Lt. M. H. Best Lt. A. F. Townsend 2 Lt. W. C. Weston Lt. P. D. Phillips 2 Lt. P. H. Kemp

Capt. L. R. Boyd Capt. G. Wheeler Capt. W. Graves, M.C. Lt. J. Dymoke Lt. E. P. Spencer
Capt. J. K. Wighton Capt. J. Bedford Lt. C. R. Harness Lt. R. E. Elliott Lt. W. F. Tomlin

Capt. P. J. Corser Major N. Corry Lt. Col. R. H. L. Oulton Major D. J. Joyce Lt. (Q.-M.) L. L. Ferguson
Major J. D. Drabble Major W. J. R. Cragg Capt. R. H. Taylor Major R. G. Young

67

APPENDIX "A".

1st BATTALION THE LINCOLNSHIRE REGIMENT.

HONOURS AND AWARDS.

BURMA, 1943-1945.

1.—Total of Honours and Awards gained by Officers and Men serving with the 1st Battalion The Lincolnshire Regiment in Burma :—

V.C.	1
D.S.O.	1
O.B.E.	1
M.C.	8
M.B.E.	3
D.C.M.	5
M.M.	12
" Mentions " ..	39
Certificate of Gallantry	1

2.—Nominal Roll of those who received Honours and Awards for Gallantry and Distinguished Service in Burma, 1943-1945 :—

OFFICERS :

V.C.

Capt. (A/Major) C. F. Hoey, M.C.   Immediate.

D.S.O.

Major (T/Lt. Col.) C. A. C. Sinker.   Immediate.

O.B.E.

Capt. (T/Lt. Col.) D. P. St.C. Roissier.

M.C.

Capt. (A/Major) C. F. Hoey.
Capt. (A/Major) A. W. Innes.   Immediate.
Lieut. (T/Capt.) A. Hill.
Lieut. I. B. Christison.   Immediate.
Lieut. (T/Capt.) J. R. Lawson.
Capt. J. W. R. Battram, R.A.M.C.
Capt. A. J. Pearson, R.A.Ch.D.

BAR TO M.C.

Capt. (A/Major) A. W. Innes, M.C.   Immediate.

M.B.E.

Lieut. (Q.M.) P. Tancred.
Lieut. (T/Capt.) P. E. Duval.
Lieut. (T/Major) A. N. B. Cheer.

MENTIONED IN DESPATCHES.

Major (T/Lt. Col.) C. A. C. Sinker, D.S.O. (Twice).
Capt. (T/Major) C. F. Hoey, V.C., M.C.
Lieut. (A/Capt.) D. J. Wright.
Lieut. (T/Major) J. W. Giardelli.
Lieut. (Q.M.) P. Tancred, M.B.E.
Lieut. Snelling.
Lieut. C. J. H. D. Page.
Lieut. P. V. Poole.
Lieut. (A/Major) P. E. Duval, M.B.E.
Lieut. (T/Major) J. B. Munroe.
Capt. (T/Lt. Col.) D. P. St.C. Roissier, O.B.E.
Capt. B. R. Williams, R.A.Ch.D.

OTHER RANKS.

D.C.M.

4802362 Sgt. G. Boyle.
6399689 Pte. H. Clout. Immediate.
4801400 Pte. F. M. Brown.

BAR TO D.C.M.

4802362 Sgt. G. Boyle, D.C.M.

M.M.

5681246 Pte. P. Neilus.
4802700 Cpl. C. Pennington. Immediate.
6027911 Sgt. H. Farrow. Immediate.
6149792 Pte. S. J. Fahrner. Immediate.
4807340 L/Cpl. G. Payne. Immediate.
4343437 Sgt. G. V. Snelling.
4029101 Sgt. A. Palmer. Immediate.
14440282 Pte. L. Barker. Immediate.
4799084 C.S.M. W. Oscroft. Immediate.
4806467 Cpl. H. R. Atkinson.
5836401 Pte. L. C. Haynes.

BAR TO M.M.

3651777 Sgt. J. Boughey, M.M. Immediate.

MENTIONED IN DESPATCHES.

4801465 Pte. E. Burke.
4801515 Pte. W. Paley.
4802589 Pte. J. Priestley.
 813412 C.S.M. C. Parker.
4804063 Cpl. E. Harris.
4806644 Cpl. A. Lambert.
4804198 Sgt. S. Papworth.
6006885 Sgt. F. Carter. (Twice).
3060177 Sgt. H. Kennedy.
4802428 L/Cpl. E. W. Mayfield.
4349583 Pte. C. Clappison.
6149619 Sgt. J. E. Hunt.
4036636 L/Cpl. D. E. Wright. (Twice).
4806467 Sgt. S. Wright.

```
4746422   L/Cpl. A. Garner.
5621458   Pte. R. Sampson.
6297520   Sgt. A. R. Housden.
4345337   L/Cpl. A. Ollier.
6197209   C/Sgt. A. Young.
4804384   Sgt. C. Fulcher.
14435125   Cpl. A. Brandrith.
4802802   Cpl. A. Morton.
4797443   Cpl. C. Holmes.
G.S.F./4118 Sweeper Antoo (son of Mata Box).
```

CERTIFICATE OF GALLANTRY.

```
4616351   Pte. J. Rodgers.
```

APPENDIX "B".

NOMINAL ROLL OF OFFICERS AND MEN

OF THE

1st BATTALION THE LINCOLNSHIRE REGIMENT
WHO PAID THE SUPREME SACRIFICE IN THE BURMA CAMPAIGN
UP TO 20TH MAY, 1945.

Leiut. H. B. Ayres.
Lieut. A. C. J. Barnes.
Leiut. J. F. Berry.
Lieut. L. C. Bustard.
Lieut. J. Gilbert.
Lieut. W. A. Greenshields.
Lieut. J. V. Heaton.
Major A. Hill, M.C.
Major C. F. Hoey, V.C., M.C.
Lieut. J. A. M. Hutton.
Lieut. R. A. G. Lines.
Lieut. E. J. Miles.
Lieut. J. Morris.
Lieut. Whitehouse.
Lieut. A. B. Wilkinson.
Capt. G. R. V. Powell.

Pte. Addison, G. W.	Cpl. Borg, F.	Pte. Carr, H. L.
L/Cpl. Ashbourne, R.	Pte. Boutell, J.	„ Chambers, F.
Pte. Bailey, H.	L/Cpl. Bramford, J.	„ Clark, G. W.
„ Bark, G.	Cpl. Bray, J.	„ Clarke, S.
„ Barker, L., M.M.	„ Brearley, W.	„ Clish, T.
„ Barrett, R.	Pte. Brewin, G. H.	Sgt. Cook, N.
„ Barrett, C.	Cpl. Brotherton, H.	Pte. Corlett, K.
„ Barrick, T.	Pte. Broughton, J.	„ Cowles, H.
„ Basford, B.	„ Brown, C. D.	„ Cresswell, A. W.
„ Beekon, E.	„ Burden, C. J.	L/Cpl. Cross, H.
Cpl. Bird, F. G.	„ Burton, A.	Pte. Cruise, T.
Pte. Blackburn, A.	„ Burton, A. T.	„ Dady, D. S.
„ Bliss, A.	„ Camp, R.	Cpl. Davies, J.
„ Bloss, L.	„ Carr, A.	Pte. Dickinson, E.

Pte. Duerden, J.
Cpl. Dunn, G.
Pte. Dwyer, J.
  „ Edmonds, J.
Sgt. Edwards, W. T.
Pte. Ellis, W.
  „ Ferguson W.
  „ Fitzsimmons, A. R.
  „ Ford, H. E.
  „ Foulds, A.
  „ Fox, R.
  „ Genders, J.
  „ Gill, L.
  „ Gist, R. W.
  „ Goodwin, R.
  „ Gough, V.
  „ Graham, E.
  „ Gregory, W.
  „ Hadley, F.
  „ Handshaw, J. G.
  „ Harris, A. E.
  „ Harrison, E.
  „ Heathfield, J.
  „ Heeds, C. W.
  „ Hibbert, G.
  „ Hollingsworth, A.
  „ Holmes, J. W.
  „ Holmes, V.
  „ Horsefield, C.
  „ Horton, A.
  „ Howell, R. P.
  „ Humber, E. H.
Sgt. Hunt, J. E.
Pte. Hunter, T.
  „ Hurst, F.
  „ Jackson, G.
  „ James, F.
  „ Jennings, W.
Cpl. Jewkes, J.
Pte. Johns, E.
  „ Johnson, F.
  „ Jones, D.
  „ Kahn, J.
Sgt. Kennedy, H.
  „ Kilburn, E.
L Sgt. Kitchen, W.
Pte. Ledger, H.
  „ Lee, T.
  „ Lee, W.
L Cpl. Lockley, W. E.
Sgt. Lockley, W.
Pte. Ludlain, H.
L/Sgt. Lyon, J.

Pte. McBeath, A.
  „ McDonald, A.
  „ McInnes, M.
  „ McKenna, R.
Sgt. Makepiece, G.
Pte. Malin, A.
  „ Mansfield
  „ Marsden, C. A. E.
  „ Mellor, E.
  „ Millson, E. A.
  „ Milne, A.
  „ Mison, H.
  „ Moody, G. W.
  „ Moore, A. U.
  „ Morris, D.
  „ Morris, F.
  „ Moulton, A.
  „ Neal, A. E.
  „ Nicholson, F.
  „ Nunn, R.
Cpl. Oakley, F.
L Cpl. Oram, H.
  „ Osborne, J.
Cpl. Osbourne, H.
Pte. Ovington, G.
  „ Parham, W.
  „ Parkinson, J.
  „ Passant, J.
  „ Pettit, J.
  „ Phillips, J. T.
  „ Piff, G.
L/Cpl. Pilsworth, E.
Pte. Priddey, R.
  „ Pudge, L. G.
L Cpl. Pugh, H.
Sgt. Pulford, N. F.
Pte. Rawlinson, J. A.
  „ Renaut, H. V.
  „ Rhodes, P.
  „ Richards, L.
L Cpl. Roberts, W.
Pte. Robinson, J.
  „ Rook, W.
  „ Rowbottom, E.
  „ Rowley, W.
  „ Rushbrook, J.
Cpl. Ryan, P. J.
Pte. Saxton, N. J.
  „ Scott, J.
  „ Scroop, F.
  „ Seale, W.
  „ Sharpe, G.
  „ Sharpe, H.

Pte. Sibcy, J. S.
  „ Slinger, R.
  „ Smith, A. W.
  „ Smith, J.
Sgt. Smith, R. H.
Pte. Smith, D.
  „ Spinks, J.
  „ Stamp, R.
Cpl. Steede, J.
Pte. Stephenson, H.
  „ Stiff, J.
  „ Stinson, W.
  „ Stockton, C. C.
  „ Stones, A. L.
  „ Strong, S.
  „ Sullivan, D. P.
  „ Sutton, F.
  „ Thompson, S. F.
  „ Toynton, G.
  „ Triggs, L.
Cpl. Turner, J.
Pte. Turner, R.
  „ Turton, A.
  „ Wade, A.
  „ Walsh, J.
L/Cpl. Washbourne, R.
Pte. Watkins, J.
  „ Wells, L.
  „ Welsh, L.
  „ Weston, W.
  „ Whitehand, S.
  „ Whitehead, J.
  „ Whitfield, S.
  „ Wiggins, A.
  „ Wilkinson, M.
Sgt. Williams, C.
L/Cpl. Williams, W.
Pte. Wilmott, F.
  „ Wilson, J. P.
  „ Withers, T.
  „ Wood, H.
  „ Woods, D.
  „ Wright, S.
L/Cpl. Yarrick, E.
Pte. Youngman, W.

INDIAN PERSONNEL POSTED TO 1/LINCOLNS.

N.C.E. Pertab

Total: 16 Officers
       195 Other Ranks
       1 N.C.E.

Personnel of 1st Battalion the Lincolnshire Regiment who have paid the supreme sacrifice since coming out of Burma and entering Sumatra :—

    Pte. E. Jacques.   Cpl. H. Richards.   *Total:* 2 Other Ranks.

Casualties from 10th October, 1945 (Landing on Sumatra) :—

Pte. H. Burkinshaw	Pte. H. Larner
L/Cpl. H. Gell	Pte. E. Naylor
L/Cpl. H. James	Pte. A. Purple. *Total:* 7 Other Ranks.
Pte. S. Lane	

APPENDIX " C ".

NOMINAL ROLL OF OFFICERS

OF

1st BATTALION THE LINCOLNSHIRE REGIMENT
WHO EMBARKED RAMREE ISLAND
FOR THE LANDING ON RANGOON, 2nd MAY, 1945.

BATTALION HEADQUARTERS, AND HEADQUARTERS COMPANY.

Comd.	Lt.-Col. D. P. St.C. Roissier, O.B.E.
2 I/c.	Major G. Davey.
Adjutant	Capt. H. C. West.
I.O.	Capt. I. A. North.
Coy. Comd.	Major P. E. Duval, M.B.E.
Sig. Offr.	Capt. D. V. Poole.
Def. Pl. Comd.	Lieut. J. K. Wighton.

"A "COMPANY.

Coy. Comd.	Major I. B. Christison, M.C.
2 I/c. Coy.	Capt. M. G. Beattie.
Pl. Comds.	Lieut W. Scarr.
	Lieut. T. M. Dennehy.
	Lieut. W. V. T. Little.

" B " COMPANY.

Coy. Comd.	Major K. Neville.
2 I/c. Coy.	Capt. R. M. Finch.
Pl. Comds.	Lieut. E. White.
	Lieut. W. B. Murphy.
	Lieut. I. R. Boyd.

" C " COMPANY.

Coy. Comd.	Major J. B. Tucker.
2 I/c. Coy.	Capt. L. V. Powell.
Pl. Comds.	Lieut. L. C. Parker.
	Lieut. R. W. K. Parlby.
	Lieut. H. Smith.

" D " COMPANY.

Coy. Comdr.	Capt. J. W. Giardelli.
2 I/c. Coy.	Lieut. C. L. Beale.
Pl. Comds.	Lieut. W. G. N. Dunbar.
	Lieut. W. Craven.

" ADMIN." COMPANY.

Coy. Comd.	
2 I/c. Coy.	Capt. G. R. Bell.
Q.M.	Lieut. N. Seaton.
Padre	Capt. (Rev.) W. G. A. Wright, R.A.Ch.D
R.M.O.	Capt. C. Cameron-Mowat, R.A.M.C.

APPENDIX "D".

NOMINAL ROLL OF OFFICERS

OF

1st BATTALION, THE LINCOLNSHIRE REGIMENT
WHO EMBARKED MADRAS FOR SUMATRA ON 4TH OCTOBER, 1945.

BATTALION HEADQUARTERS, AND HEADQUARTERS COMPANY.

Comd.	Lt.-Col. D. P. St. C. Roissier, O.B.E.
2 I/c.	
Adjutant	Capt. H. C. West.
I.O.	Capt. J. D. Drabble.
H.Q. Coy. Comd.	Capt. T. R. Johnson (Sig. Officer).
Mortar Offir.	Capt. D. F. Long (A Adjt.)
Def. Pl.	Lieut. F. J. D. Ferguson.

"A" COMPANY.

Coy. Comd.	Major M. G. B. Beattie.
2 I/c.	Capt. W. V. T. Little.
Pl. Comds.	Lieut. R. G. Young.
	Lieut. S. T. Hawley.

"B" COMPANY.

Coy. Comd.	Major N. B. F. Corry.
2 I/c.	Capt. E. White.
Pl. Comds.	Lieut. W. B. Murphy.
	Lieut. I. R. Boyd.

"C" COMPANY.

Coy. Comd.	Major L. V. Powell.
2 I/c.	Capt. P. E. Gartner, M.C.
Pl. Comds.	Lieut. R. W. K. Parlby.
	Lieut. W. H. Froggatt.
	Lieut. H. Smith.

"D" COMPANY.

Coy. Comd.	Major J. W. Giardelli.
2 I c.	Capt. C. L. Beale.
Pl. Comds.	Lieut. J. K. E. Sawkins.
	Lieut. G. G. Aked.
	Lieut. W. Craven.

"ADMIN." COMPANY.

Coy. Comd.	Capt. R. M. Finch.
M.T.O.	Capt. J. K. Wighton.
Padre	Capt. (Rev.) W. G. A. Wright, R.A.Ch.D.
R.M.O.	Capt. C. Cameron-Mowat, R.A.M.C.

APPENDIX "E"

DO from

Maj. Gen. R. C. O. Hedley, D.S.O.

Comd. 26 Ind. Div.

H.Q. 26 Indian Division

South East Asia Command.

14th November, 1946.

Dear General Priestman,

I wonder if you remember me as a G.C. in No. 4 Company in 1920 ?   Many years have passed and much has happened since then.   Before the war I returned to the R.M.C. as an Instructor, and once again spent my time in No. 4 Company.

I was in or near Burma for the last three years of the War, and was lucky enough to get command of 26th Indian Division in Sumatra at the end of last January.   Now we are packing our bags, and I return to India in three days' time to disband the Division in Ranchi, which will be my address for the next two months.

The 1st Battalion the Lincolnshire Regiment were in this Division for four years, and have just gone over to Malaya.   They have been the only British Regiment to have served more or less continuously in 26th Indian Division.   I have been extremely glad to have them here, and they have done a very good job.   Conditions have been anything but pleasant, and movement has been restricted to the inside of our perimeters.   Many British units might well have got thoroughly fed up, and said so in no uncertain terms, but the Lincolns have always made the best of it.   They have suffered through release, the lack of reinforcements and heavy duties, but they have never faltered.

Sumatra has not been allowed to appear much in the news, but I have had between 15,000 and 20,000 troops under my command all the time.   During our one year here, we have had 300 battle casualties, so it has not been exactly a picnic.

It has been a great pleasure to have such a sound, reliable and cheerful Battalion under my command, and I thought that you would like to know how well they have done.   I enclose a copy of my farewell order.

Bill Roissier will, no doubt, have kept you in the picture about the Battalion and its doings—I imagine that he is now on his way home.   I saw Oulton for a few minutes at the airfield here en route for Palembang.

I hope all goes well with you.

Yours very sincerely,

R. C. OSBORNE HEDLEY.

To Maj. Gen. J. H. T. Priestman, C.B.E., D.S.O., M.C.,

Kennelwood,

Hatfield, Herts,

England.

APPENDIX "F".

THE STORY OF "SGT." WIMPEY AND "SGT." TWOPENCE.

My real name is Hyder Ali and I was born in the village of Matabonga in East Bengal. My father was a peasant and he worked sometimes in the salt trade.   He has since died of dysentery.   My mother is still alive and I have three sisters and one younger brother.

During the Bengal famine of 1942 there was a shortage of food in my village and my parents went to Maundaw where they received Army Ration Cards and got a daily ration of rice at the jetty. At this time they lived in the house of a Bengali who was connected with the Army. When the Japs reached the Indian frontier my family went back into Bengal but food was still very short and my parents could not keep me. I was picked up and fed and cared for by British Troops because my parents did not want me as they had no food to give me. Pte. Holinshed—who has gone home—of the Lincolnshire Regt., looked after me, and when the Regiment reached Chittagong I was put in the Quartermaster's Stores.

From this point onwards Wimpey's story is the same as that of Twopence.

I do not remember the name of the village in Burma where I was born but I remember living in a brick house and I think my father had much property. My real name is Meah Lal. I have now no father or mother or brothers or sisters. My father and mother were killed by Japanese bombs and machine guns. When the Japanese attacked they tried to kill me and they fired at me with a machine gun but I hid in a trench. Then I ran again and they fired about six shots with rifles but missed me. I ran and ran and finally hid in a hole in the ground. In this hole I found some B.O.R's, and I wanted to run away again but I was so afraid of the Japanese that I stayed. The B.O.R's had a wireless set and one of them who could speak Japanese was always "listening-in."

Then I was sent back over a big sea (River ?) to India. An Indian took me in his boat in which he had a Bren gun. It was very dangerous but I got back safely to the British lines.

Then I was walking one day by myself in the jungle when a big officer saw me and called me to him. He was Lt. Miles of the Lincolnshire Regiment and he took me to live with him. I used to eat in the Officers Mess and I knew Major Horn, Major Wright and Colonel Sinclair (Sinker).

Lt. Miles was very good to me and I used to go on patrol with him to catch Indian spies being smuggled across the river at night. He showed me how to use guns and one night when a boat refused to stop when ordered he told me to fire at it with a Bren gun. I hit it and it sank and two Japs started to swim ashore. One of the Japs raised a revolver to shoot at Lt. Miles as he swam ashore, but I fired and hit him and he was washed away by the current. The other landed and was taken to hospital. Lt. Miles said that I saved his life. Lt. Miles was killed later by machine gun bullets.

One day I heard that Wimpey was with the Lincolnshire Regt. too and that he was to be sent away as no one would look after him, but it was arranged for us to live in the Q.M. stores.

The Lincolns moved from Chittagong to Barrabakun, then to Cox's Bazaar (?) and to many other places. At last we went to Bangalore and from Bangalore we came to Nasik Road Camp. This happened about 11 months ago (*i.e.*, November, 1945). When the Lincolns went to Java (?) we were left at Nasik Road Camp.

GENERAL NOTES.

The age of the boys is doubtful. Both say they have been in the Army 3½ years and Twopence says he was six when his parents were killed. It has therefore been necessary to fix their ages as nearly as possible and to allot them birthdays.

Sgt. Wimpey will be nine years of age on December 14th, 1946 (the birthday of King George VI).

Sgt. Twopence will be ten years of age on January 24th, 1947 (the birthday of the writer).

Incidentally, Twopence is a Hindu and Wimpey a Muslim but both are now being taught the elements of Christianity. Wimpey hopes to join the Royal Navy and Twopence to join the Royal Air Force. Wimpey says that in the Navy one does not have to work so hard as in the Army.

REGIMENTAL HISTORIES OF THE BRITISH ARMY

A SELECTION OF N&MP REPRINTED TITLES
ALWAYS AVAILABLE ALWAYS IN PRINT

READ THE REAL HISTORY OF THE SECOND WORLD WAR IN THE STORIES OF THE REGIMENTS, CORPS, DIVISIONS, & BATTALIONS THAT FOUGHT IT.

NAVAL & MILITARY
WWW.NAVAL-MILITARY-PRESS.COM
PRESS

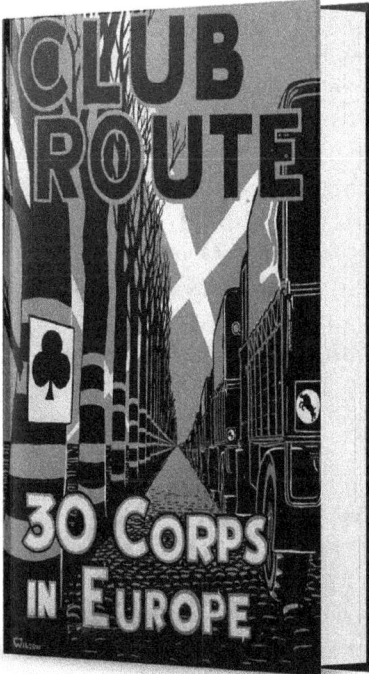

CLUB ROUTE IN EUROPE
The Story of 30 Corps in the European Campaign.
9781783311033

30 Corps was heavily involved in the closing campaigns of the Second World War in Europe, starting when its 50th (Northumbrian) Division landed on Gold Beach on D-day. It helped to clear the Cotentin peninsular in Operation Bluecoat and, after General Brian Horrocks took over command, it took part in Operation Market Garden at Arnhem, and the crossing of the Rhine into the German heartland. A superb unit history of these often difficult and bloody operations.

SEVENTH ARMOURED DIVISION
October 1938 - May 1943
9781474539180

2nd BATTALION SOUTH WALES BORDERS 24th REGIMENT
D-DAY TO VE-DAY
9781474539012

Describing the campaign from D-Day onwards, this excellent contemporary battalion history is divided into two parts. The first contains an outline of the activities of the 2/24th during the campaign in Europe from D-Day to VE-Day, and the second is a detailed narrative of some of the more important actions in which the battalion fought. Complete with a list of awards. Originally printed in Hamburg in 1945.

49 (WEST RIDING) RECONNAISSANCE REGIMENT
Royal Armoured Corps - Summary of Operations June 1944 to May 1945
9781474536677

Rare Reconnaissance unit history that was completed immediately after the war had ended. Following the D-Day invasions, the 49th Reconnaissance Regiment fought as Montgomery's left flank, and played vital roles in the capture of Arnhem, and the liberation of Holland. They are honoured annually in Utrecht to this day. The book is completed with 2 good coloured maps.

THE HISTORY OF THE CORPS OF ROYAL MILITARY POLICE
9781783310951

Excellent history of this corps, almost entirely devoted to WW2 on all fronts, including Middle East, North-West Europe and Burma. Complete with a Roll of Honour.

THE STORY OF THE 79th ARMOURED DIVISION OCTOBER 1942 - JUNE 1945
9781783310395

A magnificent and fully illustrated official history of Britain's 79th Armoured Division - the specialised unit which developed and operated 'Hobart's Funnies', the adapted tanks which carried out a range of tasks on D-day and after ranging from mine clearance to bridge laying. Follows the unit from its formation to victory in Europe.

HISTORY OF THE ARGYLL & SUTHERLAND HIGHLANDERS 7th BATTALION
From El Alamein To Germany
9781781519653

THE ESSEX REGIMENT 1929 - 1950
9781781519813

Comprehensive history of both regular & territorial force battalions, mainly Middle East (inc. Tobruk & Alamein), North-West Europe & 1st Bn. with Chindits in Burma 1944. Rolls of Honour and awards.

HISTORY OF THE IRISH GUARDS IN THE SECOND WORLD WAR
9781474537094

A fine history of a proud regiment; The Irish Guards played their part gallantly during campaigns in Europe, North Africa and Italy during the Second World War, claiming two Victoria Cross recipients during that conflict. The basis of this history was the War Diaries kept by Battalion Intelligence Officers, along with individual records and papers. A Roll of Honour, Honours Awards down to Military Medal, and 22 good maps complete this very good WW2 Regimental.

ALGIERS TO AUSTRIA
The 78th Division in the Second World War
9781783310265

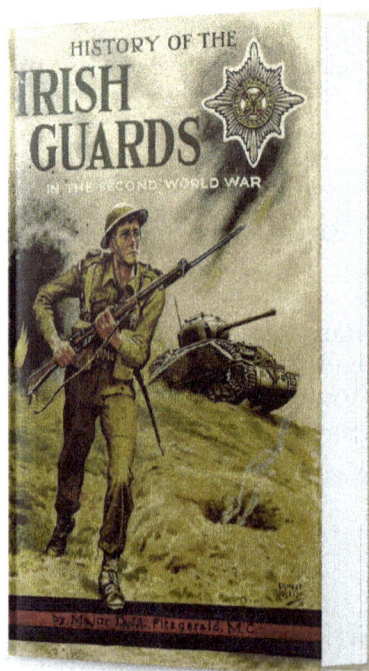

OPERATIONS OF THE EIGHTH CORPS
The River Rhine to the Baltic Sea. A narrative account of the pursuit and final defeat of the German Armed Forces March-May 1945.
9781474538176

THE HISTORY OF THE 51st HIGHLAND DIVISION 1939-1945
9781474536660

The 51st Highland Division fought and lost in France in 1940, was reborn, and fought and won in the North African desert, Sicily and finally in North Western Europe from D-Day to the end of the war. As a division the men earned the respect of friend and foe alike, and this is their story. Amply illustrated with 36 photographs, 18 maps and battle plans (many coloured) that help the reader to follow the course of the conflict. A good index (persons, units and place names) and a statistical battle casualties list complete this good WW2 Divisional History

THE HISTORY OF THE FIFTEENTH SCOTTISH DIVISION 1939-1945
9781783310852

Formed at the outbreak of war in September 1939, the 15th (Scottish) division served in North-western Europe after landing in Normandy soon after D-day on 14 June 1944 . It fought on the Odon River, at Caen, Caumont, Mont Pincon, the Nederrijn, the Rhineland, and across the Rhine. On April 10, 1946, the division was disbanded. The total number of casualties it sustained during the 12 months of fighting was 11,772.

THE STORY OF THE ROYAL ARMY SERVICE CORPS, 1939-1945
9781474538251

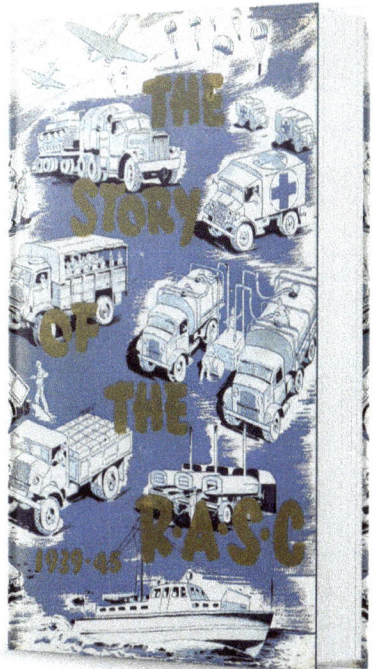

A complete history of the RASC in all theatres throughout the Second World War. This a model unit history originally published under the direction of the Institution of the Royal Army Service Corps, it is excellently produced, and arranged by theatre of war. The narrative is full with technical information, and the many photographic plates record visually British military vehicles in service situations.